Consuming Life

To Ann Bone,
editor supreme

Consuming Life

Zygmunt Bauman

polity

First published in 2007 by Polity Press

Reprinted in 2008

Polity Press
65 Bridge Street
Cambridge CB2 1UR, UK.

Polity Press
350 Main Street
Malden, MA 02148, USA

ISBN-13: 978-07456-3979-6
ISBN-13: 978-07456-4002-0 (pb)

A catalogue record for this book is available from the British Library.

Typeset in 11 on 13 pt Sabon
by SNP Best-set Typesetter Ltd, Hong Kong
Printed and bound in the United States of America by Maple-Vail

For further information on Polity, visit our website: www.polity.co.uk

Contents

Introduction

Or, the most closely guarded secret of the society of consumers

---

There is no worse deprivation, no worse privation, perhaps, than that of the losers in the symbolic struggle for recognition, for access to a socially recognized social being, in a word, to humanity.

Pierre Bourdieu, *Pascalian Meditations*

Consider three cases, picked up at random, of the fast changing habits of our increasingly 'wired up', or more correctly increasingly *wireless*, society.

Case One On 2 March 2006, the *Guardian* announced that 'in the past 12 months, "social networking" has gone from being the next big thing to the thing itself.'[1] Visits to the website MySpace, a year earlier the unchallenged leader in the newly invented medium of 'social networking', grew sixfold, while its rival website Spaces.MSN scored eleven times more hits than the year before, and visits to Bebo.com multiplied sixty-one times.

Highly impressive growth indeed – even if the amazing success of Bebo, a newcomer to the internet at the time of reporting, might yet prove to be a flash in the pan: as an expert on internet fashions warns, 'at least 40 per cent of this year's top ten will be nowhere this time next year.' 'The launch of a new social networking site', he explains, is 'like opening of the latest uptown bar' (just because it is *the* latest, a brand new or freshly overhauled and relaunched outfit, such an uptown bar would attract huge traffic 'before receding as certainly as the onset of the next day's hangover', passing its magnetic powers over to the 'next latest' in the never relenting relay race of the 'hottest', the latest 'talk of the town', the place where 'everybody who is somebody must be seen').

Once they get a foothold in a school or a physical or electronic neighbourhood, 'social networking' websites spread with the speed of an 'extremely virulent infection'. In no time, they've stopped being just one option among many and turned into the default address for swelling numbers of young men and women. Obviously, the inventors and promoters of electronic networking have struck a responsive chord – or touched a raw and tense nerve which has long waited for the right kind of stimulus. They may rightly boast of having satisfied a real, widespread and urgent need. And what might that need be? 'At the heart of social networking is an exchange of personal information.' Users are happy to 'reveal intimate details of their personal lives', 'to post accurate information' and 'to share photographs'. It is estimated that 61 per cent of UK teenagers aged thirteen to seventeen 'have a personal profile on a networking site' enabling 'socializing online'.[2]

In Britain, a country where the popular use of cutting-edge electronic facilities lags cyberyears behind the Far East, the users can still trust 'social networking' to manifest their freedom of choice, and even believe it to be a means of youthful rebellion and self-assertion (a supposition made all the more credible by the panic alarms which their unprecedented, web-induced and web-addressed zeal for self-exposure triggers among their security-obsessed teachers and parents day in, day out, and by the nervous reactions of the headmasters who ban the likes of Bebo from the school servers). But in South Korea, for instance, where most social life is already routinely electronically mediated (or rather where *social* life has already turned into an *electronic* life or *cyber*life, and where most 'social life' is conducted primarily in the company of a computer, iPod or mobile, and only secondarily with other fleshy beings), it is obvious to the young that they don't have even so much as a sniff of choice; where they live, living social life electronically is no longer a choice, but a 'take it or leave it' necessity. 'Social death' awaits those few who have as yet failed to link up into Cyworld, South Korea's cybermarket leader in the 'show-and-tell culture'.

It would be a grave mistake, however, to suppose that the urge towards a public display of the 'inner self' and the willingness to satisfy that urge are manifestations of a unique, purely generational, age-related urge/addiction of teenagers, keen as they naturally tend to be to get a foothold in the 'network' (a term rapidly replacing 'society' in both social-scientific discourse and popular speech) and to stay there, while not being quite sure how best to achieve that goal. The new penchant for public confession cannot be explained by 'age-specific' factors – not only by them at any rate. Eugène Enriquez recently summed up the message to be derived from the fast growing evidence gathered from all sectors of the liquid modern world of consumers:

> Provided one does not forget that what was previously invisible – everybody's share of the intimate, everybody's inner life – is now called on to be exposed on the public stage (principally on TV screens but also on the literary stage), one will comprehend that those who care for their invisibility are bound to be rejected, pushed aside, or suspected of a crime. Physical, social and psychical nudity is the order of the day.[3]

The teenagers equipped with portable electronic confessionals are simply apprentices training and trained in the art of living in a confessional society – a society notorious for effacing the boundary which once separated the private from the public, for making it a public virtue and obligation to publicly expose the private, and for wiping away from public communication anything that resists being reduced to private confidences, together with those who refuse to confide them. As Jim Gamble, the head of a watchdog agency, admitted to the *Guardian*, 'it represents everything you see in the school playground – the only difference is that in this playground, there are no teachers or police or moderators to keep an eye on what's going on.'

Case Two On the same day, though on quite a different and thematically unconnected page presided over by another editor, the *Guardian* informed its readers that 'computer systems are being used to snub you more effectively, depending on your value to the company you're calling.'[4] Computer systems mean that records can be kept of customers, marking them from '1', meaning first-class clients who are answered immediately the moment they call and are promptly put through to a senior agent, down to '3' (the 'pond life', as they have been summarily branded in the company lingo), who are put at the back of the queue – and when they are finally put through, they are connected to an agent at the bottom of the heap.

Just as in Case One, so in Case Two technology can hardly be blamed for the new practice. The new and refined software comes to the rescue of managers who *already* had a dire need to classify the growing army of the telephone callers in order to expedite the divisive and exclusionist practices which were *already* in operation but were until now performed with the help of primitive tools – DIY, home-made, or cottage-industry products which were more time-consuming and evidently less effective. As a spokesman for one of the companies supplying and servicing such systems pointed out, 'technology only really takes the processes we have in place and makes them more efficient' – which means instant and automatic, sparing the company's employees the cumbersome duty of collating information, studying records, passing judgements and taking separate decisions for every call, together with responsibility for their consequences. What, in the absence of the right technical gear, they would have to evaluate by straining their own brains and using up a lot of precious company time is the prospective profitability of the caller for the company: the volume of cash or credit at the caller's disposal, and the caller's willingness to part with it. 'Companies need to screen out the least valuable customers,' explains another executive. In other words, companies need a sort of 'negative surveillance', the Orwellian Big Brother style or a Panopticon-style surveillance in reverse, a sieve-like contraption which primarily serves the task of flushing the undesirables *away* and keeping the regulars in: recast as the ultimate effect of a cleaning job well done. They need a way to feed into the data bank the kind of information capable first and foremost of cutting out 'flawed consumers' – those weeds of the consumerist garden, people short of cash, credit cards and/or shopping enthusiasm, and otherwise immune to the blandishments of marketing. Only resourceful and eager players would be then allowed, as a result of negative selection, to stay in the consumerist game.

Case Three A few days later yet another editor, on yet another page, informed readers that Charles Clarke, the British Home Secretary, had announced a new 'points-based' immigration system 'to attract the brightest and the best'[5] and, of course, to repel and keep away all the others, even if that part of Clarke's declaration was difficult to detect in the press release version: either left out altogether or relegated to the small print. Who is the new system aimed to attract? Those with the most money to invest and the most skills to earn it. 'It will allow us to ensure', said the Home Secretary, that 'only those people with the skills that the UK needs come to this country while preventing those without these skills applying'. And how will that system work? For example Kay, a young woman from New Zealand, with a master's degree but a rather lowly and miserly paid job, failed to reach the seventy-five points that would entitle her to apply for immigration. She would need first to obtain a job offer from a British company, which would then be recorded in her favour, as a proof that her kind of skills are ones 'the UK needs'.

Charles Clarke, to be sure, would not claim originality for transferring to the selection of human beings the market rule of selecting the best commodity on the shelf. As Nicolas Sarkozy, his French equivalent and a hot contender for the next term of French presidency, has pointed out, 'selective immigration is practised by almost all the world's democracies', and he went on to demand that 'France ought to be able to choose its immigrants according to its needs.'[6]

Three cases, reported in three separate sections of the dailies and presumed to belong to quite separate realms of life, each governed by its own set of rules while supervised and run by mutually independent agencies. Cases seemingly so dissimilar, concerning people of widely different provenance, age and interests, people confronted with sharply distinct challenges and struggling to resolve quite distinct problems . . . Is there any reason for putting them next to each other and considering them as specimens of the same category, you may ask? The answer is yes, there is a reason to connect them; and it is as powerful as reasons come.

The schoolgirls and schoolboys avidly and enthusiastically putting on display their qualities in the hope of capturing attention and possibly also gaining the recognition and approval required to stay in the game of socializing; the prospective clients needing to amplify their spending records and credit limits to earn a better service; the would-be immigrants struggling to gather and supply brownie points as evidence of demand for their services in order to have their applications considered – all three categories of people, apparently so distinct, are enticed, nudged or forced to promote an attractive and desirable *commodity,* and so to try as hard as they can, and using the best means at their disposal, to enhance the market value of the goods they sell. And the commodity they are prompted to put on the market, promote and sell are *themselves.*

They are, simultaneously, ~~promoters of commodities and the commodities they promote.~~ They are, at the same time, the merchandise and their marketing agents, the goods and their travelling salespeople (and let me add that any academic who has ever applied for a teaching job or research funds will easily recognize her or his own predicament in their experience). Into whatever bracket they may be slotted by the composers of statistical tables, they all inhabit the same social space known under the name of the *market.* Under whatever rubric their preoccupations would be classified by governmental archivists or investigative journalists, the activity in which all of them are engaged (whether by choice, necessity, or most commonly both) is *marketing.* ~~The test they need to pass in order to be admitted to the social prizes they covet demands them *to recast themselves as commodities*~~: that is, as ~~products capable of catching the attention and attracting *demand* and *customers.*~~

Siegfried Kracauer was a thinker endowed with an uncanny capacity for gleaning the barely visible and still inchoate contours of future-prefiguring trends still lost in a formless mass of fleeting fads and foibles. Already in the late 1920s, when the imminent transformation of the society of producers into a society of consumers was in an embryonic or at best incipient stage and so was overlooked by less attentive and farsighted observers, he had noted:

The rush to the numerous beauty salons springs partly from existential concerns, and the use of cosmetic products is not always a luxury. For fear of being taken out of use as obsolete, ladies and gentlemen dye their hair, while forty-year-olds take up sports to keep slim. 'How can I become beautiful?' runs the title of a booklet recently launched on to the market; the newspaper advertisements for it say that it shows ways 'to stay young and beautiful both now and for ever'.[7]

The emergent habits which Kracauer recorded in the early 1920s as a noteworthy Berlin curiosity went on to spread like a forest fire, until they turned into a daily routine (or at least into a dream) all around the globe. Eighty years later Germaine Greer was already observing that 'even in the furthest reaches of north-western China, women laid aside their pyjama suits for padded bras and flirty skirts, curled and coloured their straight hair and saved up to buy cosmetics. This was called liberalization.'[8]

Half a century after Kracauer noted and described the new passions of Berlin women, another notable German thinker, Jürgen Habermas, writing at the time when the society of producers was nearing the end of its days and so benefiting from the added advantage of hindsight, presented the 'commoditization of capital and labour' as the major function, indeed the *raison d'être*, of the capitalist state. He pointed out that if the reproduction of capitalist society is accomplished through the endlessly repeated transactional encounters between capital in the role of the buyer and labour in the role of commodity, then the capitalist state must see to it that the encounters take place regularly and succeed in their purpose: that is, culminate in buying and selling transactions.

For this culmination to be reached in all or at least a decent number of the encounters, capital must be capable however of paying the current price of the commodity, be willing to pay it, and encouraged to act on that will – reassured by state-endorsed policy insurance against the risks caused by the notorious vagaries of commodity markets. Labour, on the other hand, must be kept in a spick-and-span condition, likely to attract the eye of potential buyers, meet with their approval and entice them to buy what they see. Just as in encouraging capitalists to spend their money on labour, making labour attractive to capitalist buyers was unlikely to be achieved, let alone assured, without the active cooperation of the state. Job-seekers had to be properly nourished and healthy, used to disciplined behaviour, and in possession of the skills required by the working routines of the jobs they seek.

Deficits of power and resources nowadays afflict most nation-states struggling to acquit themselves in the task of commoditization – deficits caused by the exposure of native capital to the ever more intense competition resulting from the globalization of capital, labour and commodity markets and from the planet-wide spread of modern forms of production and trade, as well as deficits caused by the fast-rising costs of the 'welfare state', that paramount and perhaps indispensable instrument of the commoditization of labour.

As it happened, on the way from a society of producers to a society of consumers the tasks involved in the commoditization and recommoditization of capital and labour went through simultaneous processes of steady, thorough and apparently irreversible, even if as yet incomplete, *deregulation* and *privatization*.

The speed and the accelerating pace of these processes have been and continue to be anything but uniform. In most (though not all) countries they seem to be much more radical in the case of labour than they have been thus far in the case of capital, whose new ventures continue to have their pumps primed – almost as a rule – from governmental coffers on a rising rather than diminishing scale. In addition, capital's ability and willingness to buy labour continue to be regularly boosted by the state, which tries hard to keep down the 'cost of labour' through dismantling the mechanisms of collective bargaining and job protection and by imposing legal brakes on the defensive actions of trade unions – and which all too often sustains the solvency of companies by taxing imports, offering tax relief on exports and subsidizing shareholders' dividends through governmental commissions paid for from public funds. To prop up, for instance, the failed promise of the White House to keep at-the-pump prices of petrol down without endangering stockholders' profits, the Bush administration confirmed as recently as February 2006 that the government will waive 7 billion dollars in royalties over the next five years (a sum estimated by some to quadruple) to encourage the American oil industry to drill for oil in the publicly owned waters of the Gulf of Mexico ('It is like subsidizing a fish to swim' was the reaction to the news of a member of the House of Representatives:

'It is indefensible to be keeping those companies on the government dole when oil and gas prices are so high').[9]

It is the task of the recommoditization of *labour* that has been thus far most affected by the twin processes of deregulation and privatization. This task is being by and large exempted from direct governmental responsibility through wholly or in part 'contracting out' to private businesses the essential institutional framework of service provision crucial for keeping labour sellable (as, for instance, in the case of schooling and housing, care in old age, and a growing number of medical services). So the overall task of sustaining the saleability of labour *en masse* is left to the private worries of individual men and women (for instance, by switching the costs of skill acquisition to private, and personal, funds), and they are now advised by politicians and cajoled by advertisers to use their own wits and resources to stay on the market, to increase their market value or not let it drop, and to earn the appreciation of prospective buyers.

Having spent several years observing at close quarters (almost as a participant) the changing patterns of employment in the most advanced sectors of the American economy, Arlie Russell Hochschild has discovered and documented trends which are strikingly similar to those found in Europe and described in great detail by Luc Boltanski and Eve Chiapello as the 'new spirit of capitalism'. The strong preference among employers for free-floating, unattached, flexible, 'generalist' and ultimately disposable employees (of a 'Jack of all trades' type, rather than being specialized and subjected to a narrowly focused training) has been the most seminal among the findings. In Hochschild's own words:

Since 1997, a new term – 'zero drag' – has begun quietly circulating in Silicon Valley, the heartland of the computer revolution in America. Originally it meant the frictionless movement of a physical object like a skate or bicycle. Then it was applied to employees who, regardless of financial incentives, easily gave up one job for another. More recently, it has come to mean 'unattached' or 'unobligated'. A dot.com employer might comment approvingly of an employee, 'He's zero drag', meaning that he's available to take on extra assignments, respond to emergency calls, or relocate any time. According to Po Bronson, a researcher of Silicon Valley culture, 'Zero drag is optimal. For a while, new applicants would jokingly be asked about their 'drag coefficient'.[10]

Living at some distance from the Valley, and/or being burdened with a wife or a child, lifts the 'drag coefficient' and lowers the applicant's chances of employment. Employers wish their future employees to swim rather than walk and to surf rather than swim. The ideal employee would be a person with no previous bonds, commitments or emotional attachments, and shunning new ones; a person ready to take on any task that comes by and prepared to instantly readjust and refocus their own inclinations, embracing new priorities and abandoning those previously acquired in short order; a person used to a setting where 'getting used to' as such – to a job, or a skill, or a way of doing things – is unwelcome and so imprudent; last but not least, a person who will leave the company when they are no longer needed, without complaint or litigation. A person, too, who considers long-term prospects, career tracks carved in stone and any kind of stability even more off-putting and frightening than their absence.

The art of the 'recommoditization' of labour in its novel, updated form is singularly unsuited to being learnt from the unwieldy, notoriously inert, tradition-bound, change-resistant and routine-loving governmental bureaucracy; and that bureaucracy is singularly unsuited to cultivating, teaching and inculcating it. The job is better left to the consumer markets, already known to thrive on and be adept in training their customers in strikingly similar arts – and it is. Shifting the task of recommoditizing labour to the market is the deepest meaning of the state's conversion to the cult of 'deregulation' and 'privatization'.

The labour market is only one of many commodity markets in which individual lives are inscribed; the market price of labour is only one of many market prices that need to be attended to, watched and calculated in individual life pursuits. In all markets, however, the same rules bind.

First, the ultimate destination of all commodities offered for sale is their consumption by buyers. Second, buyers will wish to obtain commodities for consumption if and only if consuming them promises gratification of their desires. Third, the price which the prospective consumer in search of gratification is prepared to pay for the commodities on offer will depend on the credibility of that promise and the intensity of those desires.

Meetings of prospective consumers with the prospective objects of their consumption tend to become the principal building blocks of the peculiar web of interhuman relations known for short as the 'society of consumers'. Or, rather, the existential setting that came to be known as the 'society of consumers' is distinguished by a remaking of interhuman relations on the pattern, and in the likeness, of the relations between consumers and the objects of their consumption. This remarkable feat has been achieved through the annexation and colonization by consumer markets of the space stretching between human individuals; that space in which the strings that tie humans together are plaited, and the fences that separate them are built.

In a gross distortion and perversion of the true substance of the consumerist revolution, the society of consumers is most often represented as focused around relations between the consumer firmly set in the status of the Cartesian *subject*, and the commodity cast in the role of the Cartesian *object* – even if in these representations the centre of gravity in the subject–object encounter is moved decisively from the area of contemplation to the sphere of activity. When it comes to activity, the *thinking* (perceiving, examining, comparing, calculating, relevance-ascribing, making-intelligible) Cartesian subject is faced – just as it was faced during contemplation – with a multitude of spatial objects (of perception, examination, comparison, calculation, ascription of relevance, comprehension), but it is now faced in addition with the task of *handling* them: moving, appropriating, using, discarding.

Admittedly, the degree of sovereignty commonly ascribed to the subject in narrating consumer activity is questioned time and again and cast in doubt. As Don Slater has rightly pointed out, the picture of consumers painted in the learned descriptions of the consuming life veers between the extremes of 'cultural dupes or dopes' and 'heroes of modernity'. At the first extreme, consumers are represented as anything but sovereign agents: they are shown instead to be hoodwinked by fraudulent promises, enticed, seduced, pushed and otherwise manoeuvred by blatant or surreptitious, but invariably extraneous pressures. At the other extreme, the alleged likenesses of the consumer encapsulate all the virtues for which modernity wishes to be praised – like rationality, robust autonomy, capacity for self-definition and rugged self-assertion. Such portraits represent a carrier of the 'heroic will and intelligence that could transform nature and society and bend them both to mastery by the freely and privately chosen desires of the individual'.[11]

The point, though, is that in both versions – whether they are presented as dupes of promotional hype or as heroic practitioners of the self-propelling drive to mastery – consumers are cut away from and placed outside the universe of their prospective objects of consumption. In most descriptions, the world formed and sustained by the society of consumers stays neatly divided into things *to be chosen* and their *choosers*; commodities and their consumers: things to be consumed and the humans to consume them. In fact, however, the society of consumers is what it is precisely because of being nothing of the sort; what sets it apart from other types of society is exactly the *blurring,* and ultimately the *effacing* of the divisions listed above.

In the society of consumers no one can become a subject without first turning into a commodity, and no one can keep his or her subjectness secure without perpetually resuscitating, resurrecting and replenishing the capacities expected and required of a sellable commodity. The 'subjectivity' of the 'subject', and most of what that subjectivity enables the subject to achieve, is focused on an unending effort to itself become, and remain, a sellable commodity. The most prominent feature of the society of consumers – however carefully concealed and most thoroughly covered up – is the *transformation of consumers into commodities*; or rather their dissolution into the sea of commodities in which, to quote what is perhaps the most quoted of Georg Simmel's immensely quotable propositions, the different meanings of things 'and thereby the things themselves, are experienced as insubstantial', appear 'in an evenly flat and grey tone' – while all things 'float with equal specific gravity in the constantly moving stream of money'.[12] The task of the consumers therefore, and the principal motive prompting them to engage in incessant consumer activity, is the task of lifting themselves out of that grey and flat invisibility and insubstantiality, making themselves stand out from the mass of indistinguishable objects 'floating with equal specific gravity', and so catching the eye of (blasé!) consumers . . .

The first album recorded by Corinne Bailey Rae, a 27-year-old singer born in Leeds and signed up in 2005 by an A&R man from

EMI, turned platinum in just four months.[13] An amazing event, one in a million or hundreds of millions – shooting to stardom after a brief appearance in an indie band and a job as cloakroom attendant at a Soul Club. A chance of probability no greater, perhaps still smaller than winning the lotto jackpot (but let us note that week in, week out millions go on buying lotto tickets). 'My mum teaches in a primary school,' Corinne told her interviewer, 'and when she asks the kids what they want to be when they grow up, they say, "famous". She asks them what for and they say, "Dunno, I just want to be famous." '

In those dreams, 'being famous' means no more (but no less either!) than being paraded on the front pages of thousands of magazines and millions of screens, being seen, noticed, talked about, and therefore, presumably, *desired* by many – just like those shoes or skirts or accessories that are currently displayed in glossy magazines and on TV screens and therefore seen, noticed, talked about, desired . . . 'There is more to life than the media,' observes Germaine Greer, 'but not much . . . In the information age invisibility is tantamount to death.' Constant, unstoppable recommoditization is for the commodity, and so for the consumer, what metabolism is for living organisms.

Beneath the dream of fame, another dream, a dream of no longer dissolving and staying dissolved in the grey, faceless and insipid mass of commodities, a dream of turning into a notable, noticed and coveted commodity, a talked-about commodity, a commodity standing out from the mass of commodities, a commodity impossible to overlook, to deride, to be dismissed. In a society of consumers, turning into a desirable and desired commodity is the stuff of which dreams, and fairy tales, are made.

Writing from inside the budding society of producers, Karl Marx censured the economists of his time for the fallacy of 'commodity fetishism': for their habit of overlooking or hiding human interaction, by design or by default, behind the movement of commodities; *as if* the commodities, on their own, entered relationships with each other with no human mediation. The discovery of the buying and selling of labouring capacity as the essence of 'industrial relations' hidden inside the phenomenon of the 'circulation of commodities', Marx insisted, was as shocking as it was revolutionary: a first step towards the restoration of human substance in the increasingly dehumanized reality of capitalist exploitation.

Somewhat later, Karl Polanyi would tear another hole in the illusion spun by commodity fetishism: yes, he would say, labour capacity was sold and bought *as if* it was a commodity like any other, but no, he would insist, labour capacity *was not* and *could not be* a commodity 'like' any other. The impression that labour was a commodity pure and simple could only be a gross travesty of the real state of affairs, since 'labour capacity' can't be bought or sold separately from its carriers. Unlike in the case of other commodities, the buyers can't 'take home' their purchases. What they have bought does not become their exclusive and unconditional property, and they are not free to *utere et abutere* (use or abuse) it at will, as they are in the case of their other purchases. The apparently 'purely commercial' transaction (recall Thomas Carlyle's complaint in the early nineteenth century that multifaceted human relations were reduced to a bare 'cash nexus') inevitably binds the carriers and the buyers of labour power in a *mutual* bond and tight *inter*dependency. On the labour market, a *human* relationship is born out of every *commercial* transaction; each labour contract is another refutation of commodity fetishism, and in the aftermath of each transaction proofs quickly appear of its falsehood, and of the deception or self-deception following it.

If it was the lot of *commodity fetishism* to hide from view the human, all too human substance of the society of *producers*, it is the turn of *subjectivity fetishism* to hide the commoditized, all too commoditized reality of the society of *consumers*.

'Subjectivity' in the society of consumers, just as 'commodity' in the society of producers, is (to use Bruno Latour's felicitous concept) a *faitishe* – a thoroughly human product elevated to the rank of superhuman authority through forgetting or rendering irrelevant its human, all too human origins, together with the string of human actions that led to its appearance and was the *sine qua non* condition of that appearance. In the case of the commodity in the society of producers, it was the act of buying and selling the labour capacity of producers that, by endowing it with market value, made the product of labour into a commodity – in a way not visible in (being hidden by) the appearance of an autonomous interaction of commodities. In the case of subjectivity in the society of consumers, it is the turn of the buying and selling of the tokens deployed in the construction of identity – that allegedly public expression of the 'self' which is in fact Jean Baudrillard's 'simulacrum', substituting 'representation' for what it is assumed to represent – to be effaced from the appearance of the final product.

Consumers' 'subjectivity' is made out of shopping choices – choices made by the subject and the subject's prospective purchasers; its description takes the form of the shopping list. What is assumed to be the *materialization* of the inner truth of the self is in fact an *idealization* of the material – objectified – traces of consumer choices.

Some time ago one of the ever more numerous internet dating agencies (parship.co.uk) conducted a survey which showed that in 2005 two-thirds of the single people using dating services (about 3.6 million) turned to the internet. The 'internet dating' business reached 12 million pounds in that year and that was expected to rise to 47 million by 2008.[14] In a matter of the six months preceding the survey, the proportion of singles believing they would meet the right partner on the internet grew from 35 per cent to 50 per cent – and the trend is still upwards. Commenting on such findings, the author of one of the 'spiked essays' published on the web observes:

> It reflects a fundamental shift in how people are encouraged to think about their personal relationships and organize their personal lives, with intimacy acted out in public and subject to the contractual norms one might associate with buying a car, a house, a holiday.[15]

Sharing the view expressed by another 'spiked' writer,[16] the author believes that prospective users are prompted to switch to internet services as a 'safer, more controlled option' since it allows them to avoid 'the risk and unpredictability of face-to-face encounters'. 'Fear of being alone sends people to their computers, while stranger danger encourages procrastination from real-life encounters.' But there is a price to be paid. Jonathan Keane notes the 'creeping sense of unease and abuse' that haunts people, however hard they try to avoid it, as they turn from one website to another, just as they used to turn over catalogue pages, in search of their ideal partner.[17]

Clearly, the people turning to internet agencies for help have been pampered by the user-friendly consumer market which promises to make every choice secure and every transaction one-off and without obligation, an act with 'no hidden costs', 'nothing more to pay, ever', 'no strings attached', 'no agent will call'. The side-effect (one could say, using the currently fashionable expression, the 'collateral casualty') of such a cosseted existence – minimizing risks, heavily reducing or abdicating responsibility and carrying an *a priori* neutralized subjectivity of the protagonists – has proved however to be a considerable amount of social deskilling.

The company of flesh-and-blood human beings makes the habitual clients of internet dating agencies, properly primed by commodity market practices, feel ill at ease. The sorts of commodities with which they have been trained to socialize are for touching, but have no hands to touch, are laid bare for examination, but do not return the look and do not demand the look to be returned and so abstain from exposing the viewer to scrutiny, while placidly exposing themselves to the client's examination; one can examine them all over without fearing their scrutiny of one's own eyes, those windows into the soul's most private secrets. Internet agencies derive most of their attraction from recasting the sought-after human partners as the kinds of commodities which well-trained consumers are used to confronting and know how to handle. The more seasoned and 'mature' their clients become, the more they are taken aback, confused and embarrassed when they come 'face to face' and discover that the looks must be reciprocated and that in 'transactions' they, the subjects, are also objects.

In the shops, goods come complete with answers to all the questions their prospective buyer might wish to ask before taking the decision to buy, but they themselves keep politely silent and don't ask questions, let alone embarrassing ones. Commodities confess all there is to be confessed, and more – without asking for reciprocity. They stick to the role of the Cartesian 'object' – fully docile, obedient stuff for the omnipotent subject to handle, give shape to, put to good use. By their sheer docility they elevate the buyer to the noble, flattering and ego-boosting rank of the sovereign subject, uncontested and uncompromised. Playing the role of objects impeccably and realistically enough to convince, market commodities supply and perpetually replenish the epistemological and praxiological grounding for 'subjectivity fetishism'.

As buyers, we have been properly primed by market managers and commercial scriptwriters to play the subject's role – a make-believe lived through as a living truth; play-acting performed as 'real life', but with the passage of time elbowing out that real life, stripping it on its way of all chances of return. And as more and more of life's necessities, once upon a time obtained the hard way, without the luxury of the go-between service of shopping-networks, become commoditized (the privatization of water supplies, for instance, leading unswervingly to the bottled water on shop shelves), so the foundations of 'subjectivity fetishism' are broadened and firmed up. To complete the popular, revised version of Descartes's Cogito, 'I shop therefore I am . . .', 'a subject' could and should be added. And as the time spent on shopping grows longer (physically or in thought, in flesh or electronically), the occasions to add to it multiply.

Switching to the web to choose/purchase a partner follows the much wider trend towards internet shopping. More and more people prefer to buy on websites rather than in shops. Convenience (home delivery) and petrol economy is the immediate, though only a partial, explanation. The spiritual comfort gained from replacing a shop assistant with the monitor is equally, if not yet more, important.

An encounter with a live person calls for the kinds of social skills which may be missing or prove inadequate, and a dialogue always means exposing oneself to the unknown: as if giving a hostage to fate. It is so much more reassuring to know that it is my, only my palm that holds the mouse and my, only my finger that rests on the button. No longer will it happen that an inadvertent (and uncontrolled!) grimace on my face, or a flickering but revealing expression of desire will leak out and betray to the person on the other side of the dialogue more of my inner thoughts or intentions than I am prepared to divulge.

In *Soziologie der Sinne*, 'Sociology of the Senses', Georg Simmel pointed out that the look I give another person willy-nilly uncovers my own self. The look I give the other in the hope of obtaining a glimpse of her or his state of mind and/or heart is bound itself to be expressive, and the innermost emotions which are shown in that way can't easily be bridled or camouflaged – unless I am a highly trained professional actor. It makes sense therefore to imitate the alleged habit of the ostrich of burying its head in the sand and avert or cast down my eyes: by not looking the other in the eye, I make my inner self (more to the point, my inner thoughts and emotions) invisible, inscrutable . . .

Now, in an era of desktops, laptops, palm-held devices and mobiles, most of us have more than enough sand around in which to bury our heads. No longer need we worry about the seller's superior skills of reading faces and their powers of persuasion, or our moments of weakness. My fears and hopes, desires and doubts will stay what they should be: mine and mine only. I will not rush to press the 'buy now' key and 'confirm' before I have collected, listed and pondered all 'pros' and 'cons' of each choice and weighed them against the 'pros' and 'cons' of all alternative choices. As long as I proceed in such a cautious manner, the hour of reckoning, of sentence-passing, that point of no return and regrets of 'too late to reconsider', 'no way back' and 'no starting again' is kept at arm's (or more to the point in the case of keyboard operators, at fingers') length; I am the one, the only one who stays in command and holds the steering wheel. I feel protected against the ploys and subterfuges of the unknown and impenetrable others – but also against myself, against a decision slipping out, against acting 'on the spur of the moment' in a way I might regret for – I have no way of knowing – perhaps an infinite time to come. This applies to buying a car or a lawnmower or an entertainment centre or a laptop or a holiday; why should not it apply to the purchase of partners?

And last but not least: in our world where one tempting novelty chases after another at breathtaking speed, in a world of incessant new beginnings, to travel hopefully feels much safer and much more enchanting than the prospect of arrival: the joy is all in the shopping that gratifies, while the acquisition itself, with the vision of being burdened with its possibly clumsy and awkward effects and side-effects, portends a high likelihood of frustration, sorrow and regret. And as internet shops stay open all hours, one can stretch at will the time of gratification uncontaminated by any worry of future frustrations. A shopping escapade no longer needs to be a long-planned outing – it may be broken up into a multitude of joyful moments of excitement, lavishly sprinkled over all other life pursuits, adding bright colours to even the darkest or dullest of spots.

The snag, of course, is that seeking a *partner* does not fit well into the shopping-and-buying scheme; even less does seeking a *life companion*, a partner-for-life.

The help the internet can deliver in the perpetual pre-emptive war against the risks and anxieties filling to the brim the life of a chooser in the society of choosers is bound to remain limited and 'up to a point'. It may placate somewhat the anxieties of the searcher for the duration of the search, but it won't reach beyond the moment of fulfilment to which the journey of discovery is hoped and expected to lead, and from which it is believed to derive its attraction and motive. Just like the commodity fetishism which haunted the society of producers, the subjectivity fetishism that haunts the society of consumers is ultimately grounded in an illusion.

The productive power of producers could not be separated from the producers themselves, whose inalienable power it was; an invisible, yet heavy and inescapable cost of the transaction of the buying and selling of labour was therefore a complex, multifaceted and above all *reciprocal* bond tying together the buyers and the sellers for the duration of the production process which the purchased labour force was intended to serve. That bond meant it was a foregone conclusion that there would be a long, perhaps unending chain of interest clashes, simmering antagonisms or open enmities, daily skirmishes and long-term wars of recognition. It is much the same story with the purchase of a 'pleasure force': however fully and honestly they are listed on the website of the dating agency, the wondrous joy-giving *qualities* sought by the internet surfers in their would-be partners and which they allow to guide their choices cannot be separated from the *persons* whose qualities they are, just as the labour force could not be cut off from the producers whose force it was.

Unlike the fiction electronically patched together out of a number of pre-selected attributes, the real person is endowed with a tongue to speak as much as with an ear to listen, wishes the partner-elect to look in her or his eyes as much as being willing to expose his or her own eyes to the partner's scrutiny,

has emotions waiting to be aroused as much as the capacity of
arousing them, and a biography fully of her or his own complete
with a biographically shaped character, expectations and model
of happiness: nothing remotely reminiscent of the passive, docile,
submissive and pliable Cartesian 'object'. The curse of reciprocal
aucthorship (that 'impure' blend of 'the actor' and 'the author',
in all probability unable to be purified because of the irreducible
authorial potency of all actors and the well-nigh impossibility of
'pure reiterations' of patterned moves) will call the bluff of the
illusion of 'pure subjectivity'. No amount of precautions will
change that fact, or 'cleanse' the relationship of that curse: it will
hover above the series of keen and ingenious attempts to change
it, however long they go on.

There are limits to how far the 'consumer sovereignty' promised
by the society of consumers can be stretched – impassable limits
– and from every human encounter these limits tend to emerge
fortified despite (or because of) the pressures to redraw them.

Subjectivity fetishism, just like commodity fetishism before it,
is founded on a lie, and it is so founded for much the same reason
as its predecessor was – even if the two varieties of fetishism focus
their cover-up operations on opposite sides of the subject–object
dialectics ingrained in the human existential condition. Both varieties of fetishism stumble and fall at the same obstacle: the stub-
bornness of the human subject, valiantly resisting the repetitive
attempts at its objectification.

In the society of consumers, the subject–object duality tends to
be subsumed under the duality of consumer and commodity. In
human relationships, the sovereignty of the subject is thereby
recast and represented as the sovereignty of the consumer – while
the resistance of the object, deriving from its incompletely suppressed, however rudimentary, sovereignty, is offered to perception as the inadequacy, unsoundness or defectiveness of a wrongly
chosen commodity.

Market-driven consumerism has a recipe for tackling that sort
of inconvenience: exchange of the faulty or merely imperfect and
not fully satisfying commodity for a new and improved one. The
recipe tends to be recast into a stratagem to which seasoned
consumers resort automatically and almost unreflexively, from a
learned and interiorized habit; after all, in consumer–commodity

markets the need to replace 'outdated', less than completely satisfactory and/or no longer wanted consumer objects is inscribed in the design of products and publicity campaigns calculated for the steady growth of sales. A short life expectation for a product's use in practice and proclaimed utility is included in the marketing strategy and calculation of profit: it tends to be predesigned, prescripted and instilled into consumers' practices through the apotheosis of new (today's) offers and the denigration of old (yesterday's) ones.

Principal among the consumerist ways of dealing with disaffection is disposal of the objects causing disaffection. The society of consumers devalues durability, equating the 'old' with being 'outdated', unfit for further use and destined for the rubbish tip. It is by the high rate of waste, and by shortening the time distance between the sprouting and the fading of desire, that subjectivity fetishism is kept alive and credible despite the endless series of disappointments it causes. The society of consumers is unthinkable without a thriving waste-disposal industry. Consumers are not expected to swear loyalty to the objects they obtain with the intention to consume.

The ever more common pattern of a 'pure relationship', revealed and described by Anthony Giddens in his *Transformations of Intimacy*, may be interpreted as a transplantation of that commodity–market rule to the realm of human bonds. The practice of the 'pure relationship', widely observed and sometimes eulogized in popular folklore and its mass media representation, can be visualized in the likeness of the assumed or postulated consumer sovereignty. The impact of the distinction of the partner–partner relationship from the act of purchase of ordinary consumer goods, a rather profound distinction originated by the *mutuality* of consent required for the relationship to be *initiated*, is minimized (if not made irrelevant altogether) by the codicil making the decision of *one* of the partners sufficient to *terminate* it. It is that clause which lays bare the *similarity* overriding the *difference*: in the model of a 'pure relationship', just as on the commodity markets, partners are entitled to treat each other as they treat the objects of consumption. Once permission (and the prescription) to reject and replace an object of consumption which no longer brings full satisfaction is extended to partnership relations, the partners are cast in the status of consumer objects.

Paradoxically, they find themselves so cast because of their struggle to gain and monopolize the prerogatives of the sovereign consumer . . .

Obviously, a 'pure relationship' focusing on utility and gratification is the very opposite of friendship, devotion, solidarity and love – all those 'I–Thou' relations deemed to play the role of cement in the edifice of human togetherness. Its 'purity' is measured in the last account by an absence of ethically loaded ingredients. The attraction of a 'pure relationship' is in the delegitimation of questions like (to quote Ivan Klima) 'Where is the border between the right to personal happiness and new love, on the one hand, and reckless selfishness that would break up the family and perhaps damage the children, on the other?'[18] In the last account, that attraction lies in declaring the tying and untying of human bonds to be morally 'adiaphoric' (indifferent, neutral) acts, thereby relieving the actors of responsibility for each other: that unconditional responsibility which love, for better or worse, promises and struggles to build and preserve. 'The creation of a good and lasting mutual relationship', in stark opposition to seeking enjoyment through objects of consumption, 'requires enormous effort' – a point that the 'pure relationship' emphatically denies, in the name of some other values among which the ethically fundamental responsibility for the other does not figure. What love, in stark opposition to a mere desire of satisfaction, needs however to be compared to, Klima suggests,

> is the creation of a work of art . . . That too requires imagination, total concentration, the combining of all aspects of human personality, self-sacrifice on the part of the artist, and absolute freedom. But most of all, as with artistic creation, love requires action, that is, non-routine activity and behaviour, as well as constant attention to one's partner's intrinsic nature, an effort to comprehend his or her individuality, and respect, And last but not least, it needs tolerance, the awareness that one must not impose one's outlook or ideals on one's companion or stand in the way of the other's happiness.

Love, we may say, abstains from promising an easy passage to happiness and meaning. A 'pure relationship' inspired by consumerist practices promises that passage to be easy and trouble-free, while rendering happiness and meaning hostages to fate – more like a lottery win than an act of creation and dedicated effort.

As I write these words, a remarkable study of the many faces of consumerism, edited by John Brewer and Frank Trentmann, has appeared.[19] In the introduction, the two editors draw the following conclusion from a comprehensive survey of the available approaches to the study of the phenomenon:

> We began this chapter by commenting on the remarkable richness and diversity of modern consumption and on the difficulty of accommodating such variety within a single interpretative framework . . . No single narrative of consumption, no single typology of the consumer and no monolithic version of consumer culture will suffice . . .

And they advise us, when we struggle with the daunting task of composing such a cohesive view of consumers and their life strategies, 'to recognize that markets are necessarily embedded within complex political and cultural matrixes that give acts of consumption their specific resonance and import. Only then will we be able to do justice to modern consumption in all its power and plenitude.'

How right they are. What follows is one more illustration to their thesis: another addition to uncountable cognitive perspectives from which the phenomenon of modern consumption has been scrutinized thus far. An attempt no less (though hopefully no more) partial than those it is meant to complement rather than correct, let alone replace.

In this book, I intend to propose three 'ideal types': of consumerism, the society of consumers, and consumerist culture. On the methodological grounding and cognitive significance of ideal types, see chapter 1; but it ought to be stressed here already that 'ideal types' are not snapshots or likenesses of social reality, but attempts to construct models of its essential elements and their configuration which aim to render intelligible the otherwise chaotic and scattered evidence of experience. Ideal types are not descriptions of social reality but the tools of its analysis and – hopefully – its comprehension. Their purpose is to force our picture of the society we inhabit to 'make sense'; to achieve that purpose, they deliberately postulate more homogeneity, consistency and logic in the empirical social world than daily experience makes visible and allows us to grasp. Their roots are sunk deeply in the soil of human everyday experience and practices. But in order to attain a better view of such practices, their causes and motives, they need a distance that allows them to embrace the field as a whole – so that the sight of human practices becomes more comprehensive and clearer to the analysts, also opening up, it is hoped, the causes and the motives of their actions to the actors themselves.

I am fully aware of the 'messiness' (complexity, multisidedness, heterogeneity) of reality that our common experience makes available to us. But I am also aware that models 'adequate at the level of meaning', as Max Weber would say, are indispensable for any understanding, and indeed for the very awareness of the similarities and differences, connections and discontinuities that hide behind the confusing variety of experience. The ideal types I propose here are meant to be 'thought with' and serve as instruments to 'see with'.

With the same idea in mind, I propose a number of concepts which I hope may help in grasping the new or emergent phenomena and processes that elide with the older conceptual nets – such as 'pointillist time', the 'commoditization of consumers', or 'subjectivity fetishism'. Last though not least, I attempt to record the impact of consumerist patterns of interaction and evaluation on various apparently unconnected aspects of the social setting, such as politics and democracy, social divisions and stratification, communities and partnerships, identity building, the production and use of knowledge, or value preferences.

The invasion, conquest and colonization of the web of human relations by the worldviews and behavioural patterns inspired by and made to the measure of commodity markets, and the sources of resentment, dissent and occasional resistance to the occupying forces, as well as the question of impassable limits (if any) to the occupants' rule, are the main themes of this book. The social forms and culture of contemporary living are scrutinized once more and reinterpreted in the light of those themes.

Inevitably, the story intended to be told here will be inconclusive – indeed, open-ended – as all reports from the battlefield are bound to be.

1

Consumerism versus Consumption

Apparently, consumption is a banal, indeed trivial affair. We all do it daily, on occasions in a festive manner, when throwing a party, celebrating an important event or rewarding ourselves for a particularly impressive achievement – but most of the time matter-of-factly, one would say routinely, without much advance planning or a second thought.

Indeed, if reduced to its archetypical form of the metabolic cycle of ingesting, digesting and excreting, consumption is a permanent and irremovable condition and aspect of life, bound by neither time nor history; one of the inseparable elements of biological survival which we, humans, share with all other living organisms. Seen in that way, the phenomenon of consumption has roots as ancient as living organisms – and most certainly it is a permanent, integral part of every form of life known from historical narratives and ethnographic reports. Apparently, *plus ça change, plus c'est la même chose* . . . Whatever form of consumption is noted as typical for a specific period in human history may be depicted with no great effort as a slightly modified version of past ways. In this field, continuity seems to be the rule; ruptures, discontinuities, radical changes, not to mention revolutionary, watershed transformations, can be (and often are) disavowed as purely quantitative rather than qualitative transformations. And yet if the activity of consuming as such might leave little room for inventiveness and manoeuvre, this does not apply to the role

played and continuing to be played by consumption in past transformations and the current dynamics of the human mode of
being-in-the-world; in particular, to its place among the factors
determining the style and flavour of social life and its role as a
pattern-setter (one of many or the paramount one) of interhuman
relations.

Throughout human history, consumer activities or consumer-
related activities (production, storage, distribution and disposal of
the objects of consumption) have offered a constant supply of the
'raw material' from which the variety of forms of life and patterns
of interhuman relations could be and indeed were moulded – with
the help of cultural inventiveness driven by imagination. Most
crucially, as an extendable space opened up between the act of
production and the act of consumption, each of the two acts
acquired growing autonomy from the other – so that they could
be regulated, patterned and operated by mutually independent
sets of institutions. Following the 'Palaeolithic revolution' which
ended the hand-to-mouth gatherers' mode of existence and ushered
in the era of surplus and storage, history could be written in terms
of the ingenious ways in which that space was colonized and
administered.

It has been suggested (and this suggestion is followed and elaborated upon in the rest of this chapter) that a highly consequential
breakpoint, which, it could be argued, deserved the name of a
'consumerist revolution', arrived millennia later, with the passage
from consumption to 'consumerism', when consumption, as Colin
Campbell suggests, became 'especially important if not actually
central' to the lives of the majority of people, 'the very purpose
of existence';[1] and when 'our ability to "want", to "desire" and
"to long for", and especially our ability to experience such emotions repeatedly, actually underpins the economy' of human
togetherness.

Excursus: On the method of 'ideal types' Before we proceed, a warning
is called for, in order to pre-empt the inevitably unresolvable disputes
regarding the uniqueness or generality, or for that matter particularity
or commonality, of the analysed phenomena. It is beyond dispute that
nothing or almost nothing in human history is totally novel in the sense
of having no antecedents in the past; chains of causality may always be
stretched infinitely into the past. But it is also beyond dispute that in

various forms of life even the phenomena that can be shown to be universally present enter a somewhat different configuration – and it is the particularity of the configuration, much more than the specificity of its ingredients, that 'makes the difference'. The model of 'consumerism', as well as those of the 'society of consumers' and 'consumer culture', proposed here are what Max Weber named 'ideal types': abstractions which try to grasp the uniqueness of a configuration composed of ingredients that are by no means unique, and which separate the patterns defining that figuration from the multitude of aspects that the configuration in question shares with others. Most if not all concepts routinely used in social sciences – like 'capitalism', 'feudalism', 'free market', 'democracy', or indeed 'society', 'community', 'locality', 'organization' or 'family' – have the status of ideal types. As suggested by Weber, 'ideal types' (if properly constructed) are useful, and also indispensable, cognitive tools even if (or perhaps *because*) they deliberately throw light on certain aspects of described social reality while leaving in the shade some other aspects considered to be of lesser or only random relevance to the essential, necessary traits of a particular form of life. 'Ideal types' are not descriptions of reality: they are the tools used to analyse it. They are good for thinking; or, arguably though paradoxically, despite their abstract nature they make empirical social reality, as available to experience, describable. These tools are irreplaceable in any effort to render thoughts intelligible and to enable a coherent narrative of the abominably messy evidence of human experience. But let us recall Max Weber's own most elegant and convincing case justifying their construction and use – an argument that has lost nothing of its topicality and relevance to sociological practice:

> (S)ociological analysis both abstracts from reality and at the same time helps us to understand it, in that it shows with what degree of approximation a concrete historical phenomenon may be in one aspect 'feudal', in another 'bureaucratic', and in still another 'charismatic'. In order to give a precise meaning to these terms, it is necessary for the sociologist to formulate pure ideal types of the corresponding forms of action which in each case involve the highest possible degree of logical integration by virtue of their complete adequacy on the level of meaning. But precisely because this is true, it is probably seldom if ever that a real phenomenon can be found which corresponds exactly to any one of these ideally constructed ideal types.[2]

As long as we remember Weber's words, we may safely (if cautiously) continue to use 'pure constructs' in our struggle to make intelligible and understand admittedly 'impure' reality, while simultaneously avoiding the traps awaiting the unwary prone to confuse 'pure ideal types' with 'real phenomena'. We can proceed therefore to construct the models of consumerism, the society of consumers and consumerist culture – in the author's view precisely the tools fit for the job of understanding a crucially important aspect of the society we currently inhabit, and therefore for also the job of constructing a coherent narrative of our shared experience of that habitation.

We may say that 'consumerism' is a type of social arrangement that results from recycling mundane, permanent and so to speak 'regime-neutral' human wants, desires and longings into the *principal propelling and operating force* of society, a force that coordinates systemic reproduction, social integration, social stratification and the formation of human individuals, as well as playing a major role in the processes of individual and group self-identification and in the selection and pursuit of individual life policies. 'Consumerism' arrives when consumption takes over that linchpin role which was played by work in the society of producers. As Mary Douglas insists, 'unless we know why people need luxuries [that is, goods in excess of survival needs] and how they use them we are nowhere near taking the problems of inequality seriously.'[3]

Unlike *consumption*, primarily a trait and occupation of individual human beings, *consumerism* is an attribute of *society*. For a society to acquire that attribute the thoroughly individual capacity for wanting, desiring and longing needs to be, just as labour capacity was in the producers' society, detached ('alienated') from individuals and recycled/reified into an extraneous force which sets the 'society of consumers' in motion and keeps it on course as a specific form of human togetherness, while by the same token setting specific parameters for effective individual life strategies and otherwise manipulating the probabilities of individual choices and conduct.

All this says little as yet about the *content* of the 'consumerist revolution'. The question that needs a closer investigation is *what* do we 'want', 'desire' and 'long for', and *how* the substance of our wanting, desiring and longing is changing in the course of and as a consequence of the passage to consumerism.

It is commonly (though arguably incorrectly) thought that what men and women who have been cast in the consumerist form of life desire and long for is first and foremost the appropriation, possession and accumulation of objects, valued for the comfort and/or the esteem they are expected to bestow on their owners.

The *appropriation* and *possession* of goods ensuring (or at least promising to ensure) comfort and esteem might indeed have been the principal motive behind human wishes and longings in the society of producers, a kind of society committed to the cause of stable security and secure stability, relying for its own long-term reproduction on patterns of individual behaviour designed to follow those motives.

Indeed, the society of producers, the principal societal model of the 'solid' phase of modernity, was primarily security oriented. In its pursuit of security, it put a wager on the human desire for a reliable, trustworthy, orderly, regular, transparent, and by the same token durable, time-resistant and secure setting. Such a desire was indeed an exquisitely suitable raw material from which to construe the kinds of life strategies and behavioural patterns indispensable for servicing the 'bulk is power' and 'big is beautiful' era: an era of mass factories and mass armies, of binding rules and conformity to rule, and of bureaucratic and panoptical strategies of domination which, in their effort to elicit discipline and subordination, relied on the patterning and routinization of individual behaviour.

In that era, large volumes of spacious, heavy, stolid and immovable possessions augured a secure future, a future promising a constant supply of personal comfort, power and esteem. Bulky possessions implied or insinuated a well-anchored, durably protected and safe existence, immune to the future caprices of fate; they could be, and indeed were trusted to insure the lives of their owners against the otherwise uncontrollable vagaries of fortune. Long-term security being their major purpose and value, acquired goods were not meant to be immediately consumed; on the contrary, they were meant to be protected from impairment or dispersal and stay intact. Like the massive walls of a fortified town intended to defend the dwellers against the incalculable and unspeakable dangers suspected to be lying in ambush in the wilderness outside, they had to be guarded against wear and tear and any premature falling out of use.

In the solid modern era of the society of producers, gratification seemed indeed to reside primarily in the promise of long-term security, not in the immediate enjoyment of pleasures; that other gratification, were one to indulge in it, would leave a bitter after-taste of improvidence, if not sin. Using up, in full or in part, the consumables' potential of offering comfort and security had to be postponed, virtually indefinitely, in case they failed to deliver the principal function in their owner's mind when they were labori-ously put together, accumulated and stored as they were intended to remain – that is, the function of staying in service for as long as a need for them might arise (practically, 'till death us do part'). Only truly durable, time-resistant and time-immune possessions could offer the security craved for. Only such possessions had the inner propensity, or at least a chance, to grow in volume instead of diminishing – and only they promised to base the expectation of a secure future on ever more durable and reliable foundations through presenting their owners as worthy of trust and credit.

At the time when it was vividly described by Thorstein Veblen at the beginning of the twentieth century, 'ostentatious consump-tion' bore a meaning sharply different from its present one: it consisted in the public display of wealth with an emphasis on its solidity and durability, not in a demonstration of the facility with which pleasures can be squeezed out of acquired riches right away and on the spot, promptly using them up and digesting and relish-ing them in full, or disposing of them and destroying them potlatch-style. The profits and benefits of display rose in propor-tion to the degree of solidity, permanence and indestructibility evident in the goods displayed. Noble metals and precious jewels, the favourite objects of display, were not going to oxidize and lose their shine, being resistant to the destructive powers of time; thanks to those qualities, they stood for permanence and continu-ous reliability. So did the massive steel safes where they were stored between periodic public displays, as well as the mines, oil rigs, factories and railways which allowed a constant supply of fanciful jewellery and insured it against the danger of being sold or pawned, or the ornate palaces inside which the owners of the jewels invited their significant others to admire them at close quarters – and with envy. They were as durable as the inherited or earned social standing they stood for was wished and hoped to be.

All that made obvious sense in the solid modern society of *producers* – a society, let me repeat, which put its wager on prudence and long-term circumspection, on durability and security, and above all on durable, long-term security. But the human desire for security and dreams of an ultimate 'steady state' are not suitable to be deployed in the service of a society of *consumers*. On the road to the society of consumers, the human desire for stability has to turn, and indeed does turn, from a principal systemic asset into the system's major, perhaps potentially fatal liability, a cause of disruption or malfunction. It could hardly be otherwise, since consumerism, in sharp opposition to the preceding forms of life, associates happiness not so much with the *gratification* of needs (as its 'official transcripts' tend to imply), as with an *ever rising volume and intensity* of desires, which imply in turn prompt use and speedy replacement of the objects intended and hoped to gratify them; it combines, as Don Slater aptly put it, an insatiability of needs with the urge and imperative 'always to look to commodities for their satisfaction'.[4] New needs need new commodities; new commodities need new needs and desires; the advent of consumerism augurs the era of 'inbuilt obsolescence' of goods offered on the market and signals a spectacular rise in the waste-disposal industry . . .

An instability of desires and insatiability of needs, and the resulting proclivity for instant consumption and the instant disposal of its objects, chimes well with the new liquidity of the setting in which life pursuits have been inscribed and are bound to be conducted in the foreseeable future. A liquid modern setting is inhospitable to long-term planning, investment and storage; indeed, it strips the delay in gratification of its past sense of prudence, circumspection and, above all, reasonability. Most valuables rapidly lose their lustre and attraction, and if there is procrastination they may well become fit solely for the rubbish tip even before they have been enjoyed. And when degrees of mobility, and the capacity to grasp a fleeting chance on the run, become major factors in high standing and esteem, bulky possessions feel more like irritating ballast than a precious load.

Stephen Bertman has coined the terms 'nowist culture' and 'hurried culture' to denote the way we live in our kind of society.[5]

Apt terms indeed, and they come in particularly handy whenever we try to grasp the nature of the liquid modern phenomenon of consumerism. We can say that liquid modern consumerism is notable, more significantly than for anything else, for the (thus far unique) *renegotiation of the meaning of time.*

As lived by its members, time in the liquid modern society of consumers is neither cyclical nor linear, as it used to be for the members of other known societies. It is instead, to use Michel Maffesoli's metaphor, *pointillist*[6] – or, to deploy Nicole Aubert's almost synonymous term, *punctuated* time,[7] marked as much (if not more) by the profusion of *ruptures* and *discontinuities*, by intervals separating successive spots and breaking the links between them, than by the specific content of the spots. Pointillist time is more prominent for its inconsistency and lack of cohesion than for its elements of continuity and consistency; in this kind of time whatever continuity or causal logic may connect successive spots tends to be surmised and/or construed at the far end of the retrospective search for intelligibility and order, being as a rule conspicuously absent among the motives prompting the actors' movement between points. Pointillist time is broken up, or even pulverized, into a multitude of 'eternal instants' – events, incidents, accidents, adventures, episodes – self-enclosed monads, separate morsels, each morsel reduced to a point ever more closely approximating its geometric ideal of non-dimensionality.

As we may remember from school lessons in Euclidean geometry, points have no length, width or depth: they exist, one is tempted to say, *before* space and time; in a universe of points, space and time are yet to begin. But as we also know from experts in cosmology, such non-spatial and non-temporal points may contain an infinite potential to expand and an infinity of possibilities waiting to explode – as was testified (if we are to believe the postulates of state-of-the-art cosmogony) by that seminal point that preceded the 'big bang' which started the time/space universe. To use Maffesoli's vivid image, nowadays 'the idea of God is summed up in an eternal present that encapsulates simultaneously the past and the future'; 'Life, whether individual or social, is but a succession of presents, a collection of instants experienced with varying intensity.'[8]

Each time-point is now believed to be pregnant with the chance of another 'big bang', and successive points continue to be believed to be pregnant too, regardless what might have happened to the previous ones and despite steadily accumulating experience to show that most chances tend to be either mistakenly anticipated or missed, while most points prove to be barren and most stirrings stillborn. A map of pointillist life, had it been charted, would bear an uncanny similarity to a graveyard of imaginary, fantasized or grossly neglected and unfulfilled possibilities. Or, depending on the point of view, it would suggest a cemetery of wasted chances: in a pointillist universe, the rates of infant mortality, abortion and the miscarriage of hopes are very high.

In the pointillist time model, there is no room for the idea of 'progress' as an otherwise empty riverbed of time being slowly yet steadily filled up by human labours; or of human labours resulting in an ever more elegant and ever higher edifice, rising from foundations to roof floor by floor, each next floor laid securely on the one erected before, until the moment when the ridge piece is crowned with a wreath of flowers to mark the end of a long and diligent effort. That image is replaced by the belief that (to quote Franz Rosenzweig's statement, which was intended as a call to arms when he jotted it down in the early 1920s, but which sounds more like a prophecy when it is read again at the beginning of the twenty-first century) the ideal goal 'could and should be reached, perhaps in the next moment, or even in this very moment'.[9] Or, in Michael Löwy's recent rereading of Walter Benjamin's reinterpretation of the modern vision of the historical process, the idea of the 'time of necessity' has been replaced by the concept of the 'time of possibilities, a random time, open at any moment to the unforeseeable irruption of the new', 'a conception of history as open process, not determined in advance, in which surprises, unexpected strokes of good fortune and unforeseen opportunities may appear at any moment'.[10] Each moment, Benjamin would say, has its revolutionary potentialities. Or finally, this time in Walter Benjamin's own words, echoing the vocabulary of the ancient Hebrew prophets: 'every second is the small gateway in time through which the Messiah may come.'[11]

With the eerie power of foresight that was his trademark, Siegfried Kracauer suggested that the imminent transformation of time would follow the lines first explored in Marcel Proust's monumental study of time past and of the mode of its posthumous existence. Proust, as Kracauer found out, radically de-emphasized chronology.

> With him, it appears, history is no process at all but a hodgepodge of kaleidoscopic changes – something like clouds that gather and disperse at random . . . There is no flow of time. What does exist is a discontinuous, non-causal succession of situations, or worlds, or periods, which, in Proust's own case, must be thought of as projections or counterparts of the selves into which his being – but are we justified in assuming an identical being underneath? – successively transforms itself . . . (E)ach situation is an entity in its own right that cannot be derived from preceding ones.[12]

The appearance of a 'telos', of a destination either preselected or preordained, may only emerge retrospectively, well after the series of 'entities in their own right' have run their course; there is no knowing what kind of logic, if any, put those 'entities' beside each other in this order, rather than that quite different one. Whatever else that retrospectively construed logic might be, it shouldn't be perceived as a product of a preconceived design/ project and a trajectory of motivated action. We may say that the currently fashionable term 'unanticipated consequence' is a misnomer, since the prefix 'un' as a qualifier to 'anticipated' suggests that the phenomenon is a case of abnormality, a departure from the norm; but the unanticipated nature of the consequences of actions *is the norm*, whereas it is an overlap between the intentions behind actions and their effects that could better fit the idea of *exception*, accident or freak event. In Proust's case, Kracauer points out emphatically:

> (a)t the end of the novel, Marcel, who then becomes one with Proust, discovers that all his unconnected previous selves were actually phases or stations of a way along which he had moved without ever knowing it. Only now, after the fact, he recognizes that this way through time had a destination; that it served the single purpose of preparing him for his vocation as an artist.

Let's note however that the sudden revelation (birth) of a sense which the string of past moments carried (while failing to reveal it to those inside, or keeping it secret from them) also occurred in a 'situation', at another 'moment' just like those other, past moments – though, as it appears, a moment more advanced in the (surreptitious) process of (unanticipated and unnoticed) 'ripening', and closer to the point of the explosive unravelling of the hidden meaning of things, than the moments by which it was preceded. Let's note as well that, now as before, there was no advance warning that this moment, unlike other moments before or after, could be the moment of truth, a moment of birth (revelation) of sense – there was no telling that it would arrive until it did. Nothing in the whole of Proust's narrative thousands of pages long suggested that it would arrive . . .

In the pointillist *paintings* of Sisley, Signac or Seurat, and in some paintings by Pisarro or Utrillo, the colourful points have been arranged in meaningful figurations: once the painter completes his canvas, viewers can see the trees, the clouds, the lawns, sandy beaches, the bathers ready to immerse themselves in the river. In pointillist *time* it is the task of each 'practitioner of life' to arrange the points in meaningful configurations. Unlike in the works of pointillist painters, this is done as a rule with the benefit of hindsight. Configurations tend to be retrospectively discovered; seldom are they designed in advance – and if they are, the brushes with which the colourful blots are transferred from mental maps to canvases are seldom if ever as obedient to the eye and the hand of 'life practitioners' as they were to the great practitioners of the visual arts.

It is precisely for such reasons that the 'nowist' life tends to be a 'hurried' life. The opportunity which any of the points might contain will follow it to its grave; for that unique opportunity there will be no 'second chance'. Each point might have been lived as a fully and truly new beginning, but if there was no fast and determined spur to instant action the curtain will have fallen right after the start of the act with pretty little happening in between. Procrastination is a serial killer of chances.

Prudence suggests that for anyone wishing to catch a chance by flashing, no speed is too great; all hesitation is ill-advised since the penalty is heavy. As ignorance of what is what will surely persist until the potency of every moment has been tested in full, only a haste that pulls out all stops may – just may – balance out the profusion of false dawns and false starts. Given that vast expanses ready for new beginnings are believed to spread out ahead, with a multitude of points whose still untried 'big bang' potential has lost nothing of its mystery and therefore has not (thus far) been discredited, hope can still be salvaged from the debris of premature ends, or rather stillborn openings.

Yes, it is true that in the 'nowist' life of the denizens of the consumerist era, the motive to hurry is partly the urge to *acquire* and *collect*. But the most pressing need that makes haste truly imperative is nevertheless the necessity to *discard* and *replace*. Being burdened with heavy luggage, and particularly a kind of heavy luggage which one hesitates to abandon for reasons of sentimental attachment or an imprudently taken oath of loyalty, would reduce the chances of success to nil. 'No point in crying over spilt milk' is the latent message behind every commercial promising a new and unexplored opportunity of bliss. Either a big bang happens right now, at this very moment of the first try, or loitering at that particular point no longer makes sense and it is high time to leave it behind and move to another. As a site for a big bang, each time-point vanishes as soon as it has appeared.

In the society of producers, the advice most likely to be heard after a false start or a failed attempt would have been to 'try again, but this time harder – with more dexterity and greater application'; but not in the society of consumers. Here the tools that failed are to be abandoned rather than sharpened and applied again with greater skill, more dedication and so hopefully better effect. So when those objects of yesterday's desires and those past investments of hope break their promises and fail to deliver the instant and complete satisfaction hoped for, they should be abandoned – along with any relationships that delivered a 'bang' that was not quite as 'big' as expected. The hurry should be at its most intense when running from one (failed, about to fail, or suspected of failing) moment to another (as yet untested). One should be wary of Faust's bitter lesson of being condemned to an eternity in hell at the very moment which he wished, precisely because it was a most enjoyable one, to stay and last forever. In the 'nowist' culture, wishing time to stop is a symptom of silliness, sloth or ineptitude. It is also a punishable crime.

The consumerist economy thrives on the turnover of commodities, and is seen as booming when more money changes hands; and whenever money changes hands, some consumer products are travelling to the dump. Accordingly, in a society of consumers the pursuit of happiness – the purpose most often invoked and used as bait in marketing campaigns aimed at boosting consumers' willingness to part with their money (earned money, or money expected to be earned) – tends to be refocused from *making* things or their *appropriation* (not to mention their storage) to their *disposal* – just what is needed if the gross national product is to grow. For the consumerist economy, the previous focus, now by and large abandoned, portends the worst of worries: the stagnation, suspension or fading of buying zeal. The second focus, however, bodes rather well: another round of shopping. Unless supplemented by the urge to get rid of and discard, the urge for mere acquisition and possession would store up trouble for the future. Consumers of the consumerist society need to follow the curious habits of the inhabitants of Leonia, one of Italo Calvino's invisible cities:

> It is not so much by the things that each day are manufactured, sold, bought that you can measure Leonia's opulence, but rather by the things that each day are thrown out to make room for the new. So you begin to wonder if Leonia's true passion is really, as they say, the enjoyment of new and different things, and not, instead, the joy of expelling, discarding, cleansing itself of recurrent impurity.[13]

Big companies specializing in selling 'durable goods' have accepted as much and concede that the really scarce, and for that reason most ardently coveted and valued service is the 'cleaning job'. Its urgency grows in proportion to the growth in acquisition and possession. These days companies seldom charge their customers for *delivery*, but ever more often they add a hefty sum to the bill for the *disposal* of the 'durable' goods which the appearance of new and improved 'durable' goods has converted from a source of joy and pride into an eyesore and a stigma of shame. It is getting rid of that stigma that now conditions happiness; and happiness, as everybody would agree, needs to be paid for. Just think of the cost of packaging waste in transit from the UK, whose volume, as Lucy Siegle reports, will soon pass the 1.5 million tonnes mark.[14]

Big companies specializing in 'skin trades', that is companies selling personal services focused on clients' bodies, follow suit. What they advertise most avidly and sell with the largest financial gain is the service of excision, removal and disposal: of bodily fat, face wrinkles, acne, body odours, post-this or post-that depression, or the oodles of as yet unnamed and mysterious fluids or undigested leftovers of past feasts that have settled illegitimately inside the body and won't leave it unless they are forcibly swept out.

As to the big firms specializing in bringing people together, like, for example, the AOL internet dating service, they tend to stress the facility with which their clients, if (but of course *only* if) they use the services offered by these firms, can get rid of unwanted partners, or prevent their partners from outstaying their welcome by becoming difficult to dispose of. When offering their go-between assistance, the companies in question stress that the online dating experience is *safe* – while warning that 'if you feel uncomfortable about a member, stop contacting them. You can block them so you will not get unwanted messages.' AOL supplies a long list of such 'arrangements for a safe offline date'.

To serve all those new needs, urges, compulsions and addictions, as well as to service new mechanisms of motivation, guidance and the monitoring of human conduct, the consumerist economy has to rely on *excess* and *waste*. The prospect of containing and assimilating the unstoppably swelling mass of innovations becomes increasingly dim – perhaps downright nebulous. This is because to keep the consumerist economy going, the pace of adding to the already enormous volume of novelties is bound to overshoot any target made to the measure of already recorded demand.

In the consumerist economy, products as a rule appear first (having been invented, discovered by chance or routinely designed in R&D offices), and only then do they seek their applications. Many of them, perhaps most, quickly travel to the dump, having failed to find willing customers, or even before they start trying. But even the lucky few that manage to find or conjure up a need, desire or wish for whose gratification they might demonstrate themselves to be relevant (or eventually to become relevant) soon tend to succumb to the pressure of further 'new and improved' products (that is, products that promise to do everything the older products could do, only quicker and better – with the extra bonus of doing a few things no consumer had until then conceived of needing or thought of paying for) well before their working capacity has come to its preordained end. Most aspects of life and most gadgets servicing life multiply, as Thomas Hylland Eriksen points out,[15] at an *exponential rate*. In every case of exponential growth a point is bound to be reached sooner or later when the offer exceeds the capacity of genuine or contrived demand; more often than not, that point arrives before another, yet more dramatic point, the point at which the natural limit to supply is reached.

These pathological (and eminently wasteful) tendencies of the exponential growth of the production of goods and services might conceivably be spotted in time – be recognized for what they are and perhaps even manage to inspire remedial or preventive measures – if it were not for one more, but in many ways special process of exponential growth which results in an *excess of information*.

As Ignazio Ramonet has calculated, during the last thirty years more information has been produced in the world than during the previous 5,000 years, while 'a single copy of the Sunday edition of the *New York Times* contains more information than a cultivated person in the eighteenth century would consume during a lifetime.'[16] Just how difficult, nay impossible it would be to absorb and assimilate such a volume of currently 'available' information (a circumstance that renders most of it endemically wasteful, indeed, stillborn), can be gleaned for instance from Eriksen's observation that 'more than a half of all published journal articles in the social sciences are never quoted';[17] which suggests that more than half of the information produced by research is never read by anyone except the anonymous 'peer reviewers' and copy-editors. And let me add that since quite a few authors of scholarly studies include in their references texts they have never read (the referencing system most widely used by scholarly periodicals, and authoritatively endorsed, calls for no engagement with the substance of the referenced text and amounts in practice to mere name dropping, thereby sanctioning and greatly facilitating such a procedure), it is anybody's guess how small the fraction is of the content of the articles that ever manages to find its way into the social-scientific discourse, not to mention tangibly influencing its direction.

'There is far too much information around,' Eriksen concludes.[18] 'A crucial skill in information society consists in protecting oneself against the 99.99 per cent of the information offered that one does not want.' We may say that the line separating the meaningful message, the ostensible object of communication, from background noise, its acknowledged adversary and most noxious obstacle, has all but been washed away.

In the cut-throat competition for the scarcest of scarce resources – the attention of would-be consumers – the suppliers of would-be consumer goods, including the purveyors of information, desperately search for the scraps of the consumers' time still lying fallow, for the tiniest gaps between moments of consumption which could still be stuffed with more information. They hope that some fraction of the anonymous crowd at the receiving end of the communication channel, in the course of their desperate searches for the bits of information they need, will come by chance across the bits they don't need but which the suppliers wish them to absorb, and then that they will be sufficiently impressed or just fatigued enough to pause or slow down for the time it takes to absorb them *in lieu* of the bits they originally sought. As a result, picking up fragments of noise and converting them into meaningful messages becomes by and large a random process. 'Hypes', those products of the PR industry intended to separate desirable (read: profitable) objects of attention from non-productive (read: unprofitable) noise – like the full-page commercials announcing the premiere of a new film or a theatre production, the launching of a new book, the broadcasting of a TV show heavily subscribed to by advertisers, or the opening of a new exhibition – focus attention, for a few minutes or a few days, on a selected object of consuming desire. For a brief moment, they manage to divert, channel and condense the keen and continuous, yet usually unguided and scattered, search for 'filters', and after that short interval it is bound to continue unabated.

Since the numbers of contenders bidding for a share of the attention of prospective consumers also grow at an exponential pace, the task of filtering outgrows the capacity of filters, however, as soon as they are invented and before they are made operational. Hence the ever more common phenomenon of 'vertical stacking', a notion coined by Bill Martin to account for the amazing stockpiling of music fashions as the promoters of novelties struggle feverishly to stretch the ability to absorb of 'music market' shoppers beyond its capacity, since the few empty areas in the 'music market' get filled to the brim by the ever rising tide of new and recycled offers. Martin suggests that in the case of popular music the images of 'linear time' and 'progress' are among the most prominent victims of the information flood.[19] Counting on the short life expectation of public memory and masquerading as the latest novelties, all imaginable retro styles, together with all conceivable forms of rehashing, recycling and plagiarizing, find themselves crowded into the one limited span of the music fans' attention.

The case of popular music, however, is just one manifestation of a virtually universal tendency affecting in equal measure all areas of life serviced by the consumer industry. To quote Eriksen once more:

> Instead of ordering knowledge in tidy rows, information society offers cascades of de-contextualized signs more or less randomly connected to each other . . . Put differently: when growing amounts of information are distributed at growing speed, it becomes increasingly difficult to create narratives, orders, developmental sequences. The fragments threaten to become hegemonic. This has consequences for the ways we relate to knowledge, work and lifestyle in a wide sense.[20]

The tendency to assume a 'blasé attitude' towards knowledge, work or lifestyle (indeed, towards life as such and everything it contains) was already noted by Georg Simmel, with astonishing foresight, at the start of the last century, as surfacing first among the residents of 'metropolis', the sprawling, immense and crowded modern city:

> The essence of the blasé attitude consists in the blunting of discrimination. This does not mean that the objects are not perceived, as is the case with the half-wit, but rather that the meaning and differing values of things, and thereby the things themselves, are experienced as insubstantial. They appear to the blasé person in an evenly flat and grey tone; no one object deserves preference over any other . . . All things float with equal specific gravity in the constantly moving stream of money.[21]

An ever more salient phenomenon, strikingly similar to that discovered and analysed by Simmel under the name of the 'blasé attitude', something like a mature and fully fledged version of the tendency spotted and recorded by that uniquely insightful thinker in its early, fledgling and inchoate stage, is currently discussed under the name of 'melancholy'. Writers apt to use that term today tend to bypass Simmel's augury and sense of foreboding and reach still further back, straight to the points where the ancients, such as Aristotle, left it, and where the Renaissance thinkers, such as Ficino or Milton, rediscovered and re-examined it. As rendered by Rolland Munro, the concept of 'melancholy' in its current use 'represents not so much a state of indecision, a wavering between the choice of going one way or another, so much as it represents a backing off from the very divisions'; it stands for a 'disentanglement' from 'being attached to anything specific'. To be 'melancholic' is 'to sense the infinity of connection, but be hooked up to nothing'. In short, 'melancholy' refers to 'a form without content, a refusal from knowing just *this* or just *that*'.[22]

I would suggest that the idea of 'melancholy' stands in the last account for the generic affliction of the consumer (the *homo eligens*, by decree of the consumer society); a disturbance resulting from the fatal encounter between the obligation and compulsion to choose/the addiction to choosing, and the inability to choose. In Simmel's vocabulary, it stands for the built-in transitoriness and the contrived insubstantiality of objects that drift over, sink in and re-emerge from the rising tide of stimulation. It stands for the insubstantiality that rebounds in the behavioural code of consumers as indiscriminate, omnivorous gluttony – that most radical and ultimate form of life strategy of last resort, hedging bets in a life-setting marked by the 'pointillization' of time and by a non-availability of trustworthy criteria that could separate the relevant from the irrelevant, and the message from the noise.

That human beings have always preferred happiness to unhappiness is a banal observation, and more correctly a pleonasm, since the concept of 'happiness' in its most common uses refers to states or events which people desire to happen, while 'unhappiness' stands for states or events they desire to avoid. The concepts both of 'happiness' and 'unhappiness' signal a distance between reality as it is, and a reality wished for. For that reason, all attempts to compare degrees of happiness experienced by people living in spatially or temporally separate ways of life can only be misconceived and ultimately idle.

Indeed, if people A spent their lives in a different socio-cultural setting from that in which people B lived, it would be vain or presumptuous to pronounce whether A or B was the 'happier'. Sentiments of happiness or its absence derive from hopes and expectations, as well as from learned habits, and these are all bound to differ from one social setting to another – so a tasty meat favoured by people A may well be regarded as revolting and poisonous by people B. If they were transported to conditions known to make people A feel happy, people B might feel excruciatingly miserable, and vice versa. And, as we know from Freud, though a sudden end to a toothache may make the sufferer feel wonderfully happy, teeth that are not painful hardly ever do . . . The best we can expect from comparisons that are guilty of ignoring the factor of unshared experience is information about the selectiveness and the time-bound or place-bound nature of the proclivity to complain and the tolerance of suffering.

The issue as to whether the liquid modern consumerist revolution has made people happier or less happy than, say, people who spent their lives in the solid modern society of producers, or in the premodern era, is therefore as moot (and ultimately contentious) as an issue can be, and in all probability will remain so forever. Whatever assessment is made, it will sound convincing solely in the context of preferences specific to the *assessors*, and the limits of their imagination. Registers of blessings and banes would surely be composed according to the notions of bliss and misery dominant at the time when the inventory is made of the things thought and/or hoped to bring happiness.

The positions, experience, cognitive perspectives and value preferences of the assessors and the assessed are bound to be doubly and hopelessly out of kilter, casting doubt on any possibility of a uniform view. The assessors have never *lived* (as distinct from paying a brief visit, while retaining the special status of visitors/tourists for the duration of the trip) under conditions that are normal to the assessed – while the assessed would never have the chance to respond to the assessment, and even if they had such a (posthumous) chance, they would not be able to judge the relative virtues of a totally unfamiliar setting of which they had no first-hand experience.

The judgements one hears or reads pronounced on the relative advantages (frequent) or disadvantages (infrequent) of the capacity of the society of consumers to generate happiness are therefore devoid of cognitive value (except when they are treated as insights into the outspoken or implicit values of their authors), so one is well advised to refrain from comparative evaluations. One should focus instead on the data which may shed some light on that society's ability to live up to *its own* promise; in other words, on evaluating its performance by the values *it itself* promotes while promising to make their acquisition easy.

The value most characteristic of the society of consumers, indeed its supreme value in relation to which all the other values are called on to justify their worth, is a happy life; indeed, the society of consumers is perhaps the only society in human history to promise happiness in *earthly life*, and happiness *here and now* and in *every* successive 'now'; in short, an *instant* and *perpetual* happiness. It is also the only society that stubbornly refrains from *justifying* and/or *legitimizing* any variety of unhappiness (except the pain visited upon criminals as the 'just deserts' of their crimes), refuses to *tolerate* it and presents it as an *abomination* calling for punishment and compensation. Indeed, as in Rabelais's *Telème* or in Samuel Butler's *Erewhon*, so in the society of consumers unhappiness is a punishable crime, or at best a sinful deviation that disqualifies its bearer from bona fide membership of society.

When the question 'are you happy?' is addressed to members of a liquid modern society of consumers, its status is therefore sharply different from the same question addressed to members of societies which did not make a similar promise and commitment. The society of consumers stands and falls by the happiness of its members – to a degree unknown and hardly comprehensible to any other society on record. The answers given to the question 'are you happy?' by members of the society of consumers may legitimately be viewed as the ultimate test of its success and failure. And the verdict insinuated by such answers, collected in a large number of surveys in a large number of countries, is not at all flattering. And this on two counts.

The first: as the evidence collected by Richard Layard in his book on happiness suggests, it is only up to a certain threshold that the reported sentiment of being happy grows with increments of income. That threshold coincides with the point of gratification of the 'essential' or 'natural' 'survival needs' – that is, with the self-same motives for consumption which the society of consumers denigrates as primitive, immature or unduly traditionalist (and indeed intrinsically at odds with happiness), and which it tries hard to replace or at least marginalize by more flexible and expansive *desires* and more fanciful, impulsive *wishes*. Above that fairly modest threshold, the correlation between wealth (and so presumably the level of consumption) and happiness vanishes. Further increments of income do not add to the volume of happiness.

What such findings suggest is that contrary to the promise from on high and to popular beliefs, consumption is neither a synonym of the state of happiness nor an activity certain to cause it to arrive. Consumption viewed in Layard's terminology as a 'hedonic treadmill' is not a machine patented to turn out an ever growing volume of happiness. The contrary seems to be true: as the reports scrupulously collated by the researchers imply, entering a 'hedonic treadmill' fails to increase the sum total of satisfaction among its practitioners. The capacity of consumption to enhance happiness is fairly limited; it can't easily be stretched beyond the level of the satisfaction of the basic 'needs of existence' (in distinction from the 'needs of being' as defined by Abraham Maslow). And, more often than not, consumption proves to be altogether hapless as a 'happiness factor' when it comes to Maslow's 'needs of being' or 'self-fulfilment'.

The second: there is no evidence whatsoever that with the growth of the overall (or 'average') volume of consumption the number of people reporting that they 'feel happy' also grows. Andrew Oswald of the *Financial Times* suggests that the opposite tendency is more likely to be recorded. His conclusion is that the residents of highly developed, well-off countries with consumption-driven economies have not become happier as they've grown richer.[23] On the other hand, it may also be noted that the negative phenomena and causes of discomfort and unhappiness, such as stress or depression, long and unsocial working hours, deteriorating relationships, lack of self-confidence and nerve-breaking uncertainties about being securely settled and 'in the right', tend to increase in frequency, volume and intensity.

The case made by rising consumption as it pleads for the status of the royal road to the greater happiness of the growing numbers has not been proved, let alone closed. This case stays wide open; and as the facts of the matter are deliberated, the evidence in favour of the plaintiff becomes more dubious and thinner on the ground. As the trial proceeds, contrary evidence accumulates, proving, or at least strongly suggesting, that in opposition to the plaintiff's argument, a consumption-oriented economy actively promotes disaffection, saps confidence and deepens the sentiment of insecurity, becoming itself a source of the ambient fear it promises to cure or disperse – the fear that saturates liquid modern life and the principal cause of the liquid modern variety of unhappiness.

While consumer society rests its case on the promise to gratify human desires to an extent which no other society in the past could reach or even dream of reaching, the promise of satisfaction remains seductive only as long as the desire stays *ungratified*; more importantly, as long as the client is not '*completely* satisfied'; that is, as long as the desires that motivated and set in motion the search for gratification and prompted consumerist experiments are not believed to have been truly and fully gratified.

Just as the easily satisfied 'traditional workers' – who wouldn't agree to work more than was necessary to allow the habitual way of life to continue – were the nightmare of the budding 'society of producers', so the 'traditional consumers', guided by yesterday's familiar needs, gladly closing their eyes and plugging their ears against the blandishments and baits of the commodity market to be allowed to follow old routines and stick to their habits, would spell the death knell of the society of the consumers, of the consumer industry and of consumer markets. A low threshold for dreams, easy access to sufficient goods to reach that threshold, and a belief in objective limits, difficult or impossible to negotiate, to 'genuine' needs and 'realistic' desires: these are the most fearsome adversaries of the consumer-oriented economy and should therefore be helped into oblivion. It is precisely the *non*-satisfaction of desires, and the unshakeable, constantly renewed and reinforced conviction that each successive attempt at their satisfaction has wholly or partly failed, leaves much to be desired and could be better than it was, that are the genuine flywheels of the consumer-targeted economy.

Consumer society thrives as long as it manages to render the *non-satisfaction* of its members (and so, in its own terms, their unhappiness) *perpetual*. The explicit method of achieving such an effect is to denigrate and devalue consumer products shortly after they have been hyped into the universe of the consumers' desires. But another way to do the same thing, and yet more effectively, stays in the semi-shade and is seldom brought out into the limelight except by perceptive investigative journalists: namely, by satisfying every need/desire/want in such a fashion that they cannot but give birth to yet new needs/desires/wants. What starts as an effort to satisfy a need must end up as a compulsion or an addiction. And it does, as long as the urge to seek solutions to problems and relief from pains and anxieties in shops, and only in shops, remains an aspect of behaviour that is not just allowed, but eagerly encouraged, to condense into a habit or a strategy with no apparent alternative.

The yawning gap between promise and delivery is neither a sign of malfunction, nor a side-effect of neglect or the outcome of a mistaken calculation. *The realm of hypocrisy stretching between popular beliefs and the realities of consumers' lives is a necessary condition of a properly functioning society of consumers.* If the search of fulfilment is to go on and if new promises are to be alluring and catching, promises already made must be routinely broken and hopes of fulfilment need to be regularly frustrated. Each single promise *must* be deceitful, or at least exaggerated, lest the search grind to a halt or its zeal (and so also its intensity) fall below the level needed to keep the circulation of commodities going between factory lines, shops and rubbish bins. Without the repetitive frustration of desires, consumer demand would quickly run dry and the consumer-targeted economy would run out of steam. It is the *excess* of the sum total of promises that neutralizes the frustration caused by the imperfections or faultiness of each one of them, and allows the accumulation of frustrating experiences to stop short of sapping confidence in the ultimate effectiveness of the search.

In addition to being an economics of excess and waste, consumerism is for this reason also an *economics of deception*. Its wager is on the *irrationality* of consumers, not on their thoroughly informed and sober calculations; on arousing consumerist *emotions*, not on cultivating *reason*. Just as with excess and waste, deception does not signal a malfunction of the consumer economy. On the contrary, it is a symptom of its good health and staying firmly on the right track; a distinctive mark of the sole regime under which a society of consumers may be assured of its survival.

The discarding of successive consumer offers which were expected (promised) to satisfy the desires already aroused and others still to be induced to be born leaves behind rising mountains of dashed expectations. The mortality rate of expectations is high; in a properly functioning consumer society it must steadily rise. The life expectation of hopes is minuscule, and only an intense boosting of their fertility and an extravagantly high birth rate can save them from thinning out and being extinguished. For expectations to be kept alive and for new hopes promptly to fill the void left by the hopes already discredited and discarded, the road from the shop to the garbage bin needs to be shortened and the passage made ever more swift.

Another crucial trait of the society of consumers sets it apart from all other known arrangements for skilful and effective 'pattern maintenance' and 'tension management' (to recall Talcott Parsons's prerequisites for a 'self-equilibrating system'), including the most ingenious among them.

The society of consumers has developed, to an unprecedented degree, the capacity to absorb all and any dissent it inevitably, in common with other types of society, breeds – and then to recycle it as a major resource of its own reproduction, reinvigoration and expansion.

The society of consumers derives its animus and momentum from the disaffection it expertly produces itself. It provides a prime example of a process which Thomas Mathiesen has recently described as 'silent silencing':[24] that is, using the stratagem of 'absorption' to nip in the bud the dissent and protest generated and spread by the system – meaning that 'the attitudes and actions which in origin are transcendent' – that is, threatening the system with explosion or implosion – 'are integrated in the prevailing order in such a way that dominant interests continue to be served.

This way, they are made unthreatening to the prevailing order.' I would add: they are converted into a major resource of the reinforcement and continuous reproduction of that order.

The principal way in which that effect is repeatedly achieved would be inconceivable were it not for the liquid modern setting of the consumerist society and culture. That setting is characterized by a far advanced deregulation and de-routinization of human conduct, directly related to a weakening and/or crumbling of human bonds – often referred to as 'individualization'.[25]

The main attraction of shopping life is the offer of plentiful new starts and resurrections (chances of being 'born again'). However fraudulent and ultimately frustrating that offer might on occasion be felt to be, the strategy of continuous attention to the making and remaking of self-identity with the help of market-supplied identity kits will remain the sole credible or 'reasonable' strategy to follow in a kaleidoscopically unstable setting in which 'whole life projects' and long-term planning are not realistic propositions and are perceived as not sensible and as ill-advised. At the same time, the potentially incapacitating excess of 'objectively available' information over the ability of the mind to absorb and recycle rebounds as a constant excess of life options over the number of reincarnations tested in practice and open to scrutiny and evaluation.

The life strategy of a fully fledged and seasoned consumer is wrapped around visions of 'new dawns'; but, to follow the metaphor used by schoolboy Karl Marx, those visions are attracted like moths to the lights of domestic lamps rather than to the glare of the universal sun now hidden beyond the horizon. In a liquid modern society, utopias share the lot of all other collective undertakings that call for solidarity and cooperation: they are privatized, and ceded ('subsidiarized') to the personal concerns and responsibility of individuals. Conspicuously missing from the visions of new dawns is a change in the landscape: it is only the observer's individual position, and so her or his chance of enjoying the landscape's wonders and charms, while escaping any less prepossessing or downright repulsive and off-putting sights, that is expected to be changed and – most certainly – 'improved'.

In a book widely read and highly influential two decades ago, Colette Dowling declared that the desire to be safe, warm, and taken care of was a 'dangerous feeling'.[26] She warned the

Cinderellas of the coming age to beware of falling into its trap: in the impulse to care for others and the desire to be cared for by others, she insisted, looms the awesome danger of dependency, of losing the ability to select the currently most favourable tide for surfing, and the prowess to leap swiftly from one wave to another the moment it changes direction. As Arlie Russell Hochschild has commented, 'her fear of being dependent on another person evokes the image of the American cowboy, alone, detached, roaming free with his horse . . . On the ashes of Cinderella, then, rises a post-modern cowgirl.'[27] The most popular of the empathizing/counselling bestsellers of the day 'whisper to the reader: "Let the emotional investor beware"' . . . Dowling cautions women to 'invest in the self as a solo enterprise'. Hochschild observes:

> The commercial spirit of intimate life is made up of images that prepare the way for a paradigm of distrust . . . by offering as ideal a self well defended against getting hurt . . . The heroic acts a self can perform . . . are to detach, to leave, and to depend on and need others less . . . In many cool modern books, the author prepares us for people out there who don't need our nurturance and for people who don't or can't nurture us.

The possibility of populating the world with more caring people and inducing people to care more does not figure in the panoramas painted in the consumerist utopia. The privatized utopias of the cowboys and cowgirls of the consumerist era show instead vastly expanded 'free space' (free for *myself*, of course); a kind of empty space of which the liquid modern consumer, bent on solo performances and only on solo performances, always needs more and never has enough. The space liquid modern consumers need, and are advised from all sides to fight for and defend tooth and nail, can be conquered only by evicting other human beings – and particularly the kinds of human beings who care and/or who may need to be cared for.

The consumer market took over from solid modern bureaucracy the task of adiaphorization: the task of squeezing the 'being for' poison away from the 'being with' booster shot. It is just as Emmanuel Levinas adumbrated when he mused that rather than being a contraption making peaceful and friendly human togetherness achievable for inborn egoists (as Hobbes suggested), 'society' may be a stratagem to make a self-centred, self-referential, egotistic life attainable for endemically moral human beings – through cutting out, neutralizing or silencing that haunting 'responsibility for the Other' which is born each time the face of the Other appears; indeed, a responsibility inseparable from human togetherness . . .

As Frank Mort points out, according to the quarterly reports of the Henley Centre for Forecasting (a marketing organization servicing the consumer industries with information about the changing patterns of leisure-time use by their prospective British customers) the places at the top of the list of the preferred and most coveted pleasures have invariably been occupied for the last two decades by pastimes

> principally made available through market-based forms of provision: personal shopping, eating out, DIY and video watching. Right at the bottom of the list came politics; going to a political meeting ranked on a par with a visit to the circus as one of the British public's least likely things to do.[28]

2

Society of Consumers

If consumerist *culture* is the peculiar fashion in which the members of a society of consumers think of behaving or in which they behave 'unreflexively' – or in other words *without* thinking about what they consider to be their life purpose and what they believe to be right means of reaching it, about how they set things and acts relevant to that purpose apart from things and acts they dismiss as irrelevant, about what excites them and what leaves them lukewarm or indifferent, what attracts them and what repels, what prompts them into action and what nudges them to escape, what they desire, what they fear and at what point fears and desires balance each other out – then the *society* of consumers stands for a peculiar set of existential conditions under which the probability is high that most men and women will embrace the consumerist rather than any other culture, and that most of the time they will obey its precepts to the best of their ability.

The 'society of consumers' is a kind of society which (to recall the once popular term coined by Louis Althusser) 'interpellates' its members (that is, addresses them, hails, calls out to, appeals to, questions, but also interrupts and 'breaks in upon' them) *primarily in their capacity of consumers*. While doing that, 'society' (or whatever human agencies armed with weapons of coercion and means of persuasion hide behind this concept or image) expects to be heard, listened to and obeyed; it evaluates – rewards and penalizes – its members depending on the promptness and propriety of their response to the interpellation. As a result, the places gained or allocated on the axis of excellence/ineptitude in consumerist performance turn into the paramount stratifying factor and the principal criterion of inclusion and exclusion, as well as guiding the distribution of social esteem and stigma, and shares in public attention.

The 'society of consumers', in other words, stands for the kind of society that promotes, encourages or enforces the choice of a consumerist lifestyle and life strategy and dislikes all alternative cultural options; a society in which adapting to the precepts of consumer culture and following them strictly is, to all practical intents and purposes, the sole unquestionably approved choice; a feasible, and so also a plausible choice – and a condition of membership.

This is a remarkable turn in the course of modern history, indeed a watershed. As Frank Trentmann found when he conducted his thorough and eye-opening attempt to retrace the place occupied by the concept of consumption and consumers in the vocabulary used by successive modern thinkers to describe the emergent social reality,

> the consumer was virtually absent from eighteenth-century discourse. Significantly, it only appears in seven of the 150,000 works of the eighteenth-century collection online – twice as private customer . . . once as the customer paying an import duty on colonial goods, once as the customer suffering from traders' high prices, and . . . twice with reference to time ('the speedy consumer of hours').[1]

In all cases, as we can see, it appeared as the name of a marginal and somewhat eccentric character, certainly only obliquely relevant to the mainstream of economics, let alone the totality of daily life. No radical change in this respect occurred during the following century, in spite of a richly documented and spectacular rise in selling practices, advertising, techniques of display and, last though not least, the Arcades – the archetypes of contemporary shopping malls (those 'temples of consumption', as George Ritzer would aptly baptise them). And as late as 1910, 'the eleventh edition of the *Encyclopaedia Britannica* only found it necessary to have a short entry on "consumption", defined as wasting away in a physical sense or as a "technical term" in economics about the destruction of utilities'.

For a better part of modern history (that is, throughout the era of massive industrial plants and massive conscript armies), society 'interpellated' most of the male half of its members as primarily producers and soldiers, and almost all of the other (female) half as first and foremost their by-appointment purveyors of services.

Accordingly, obedience to command and conformity to the rule, reconciliation to the ascribed position and its acceptance as indisputable, the endurance of perpetual drudgery and a placid submission to monotonous routine, a readiness to postpone gratification and a resigned acceptance of the work ethic (meaning primarily consent to working for the work's sake, whether meaningful or meaningless)[2] – were the principal behavioural patterns most keenly trained and drilled into those members, and expected to be learned and internalized. It was the *body* of the would-be worker or soldier that counted most; their *spirit,* on the other hand, was to be silenced, and once it was numbed and thereby 'deactivated' it could be cast aside as of no consequence and so for most purposes left out of account in calculating policies and tactical moves. The society of producers and soldiers focused on the management of bodies in order to make the bulk of its members fit to inhabit, and to act in, their intended natural habitat: the factory floor and the battlefield.

In stark distinction from the society of producers/soldiers, the society of consumers focuses its training and coercing pressures, exerted on its members from their early childhood and throughout their lives, on the management of the *spirit* – leaving the management of bodies to individually undertaken DIY labour, individually supervised and coordinated by spiritually trained and coerced individuals. Such a change of focus becomes indispensable if members are to become fit to inhabit, and act in, their new natural habitat, wrapped as it is around the shopping malls where goods are sought, found and obtained, and the streets where the commodities obtained in the shops are put on public display to endow their bearers with commodity value. As Daniel Thomas Cook of the University of Illinois has summed up the new trend:

the battles waged over and around children's consumer culture are no less than battles over the nature of the person and the scope of personhood in the context of the ever-expanding reach of commerce. Children's involvement with the materials, media, images and meanings that arise from, refer to, and are entangled with the world of commerce, figures centrally in the making of persons and of moral positions in contemporary life.[3]

As soon as they learn to read, or perhaps well before, children's 'shop dependence' sets in. There are no separate drilling strategies for boys and girls; the role of consumer, unlike that of producer, is not gender-specific. In a society of consumers, *everyone* needs to be, ought to be, must be a consumer-by-vocation (that is, view and treat consumption as a vocation); in that society, consumption-seen-and-treated-as-vocation is one universal human right *and* universal human duty that knows of no exception. In this respect, the society of consumers does not recognize differences of age or gender (however counterfactually) and will not make allowances for either; nor does it (blatantly counterfactually) recognize class distinctions. From the geographic centres of the worldwide network of information highways to its furthest, however impoverished peripheries,

the poor are forced into a situation in which they either have to spend what little money or resources they have on senseless consumer objects rather than basic necessities in order to deflect total social humiliation or face the prospect of being teased and laughed at.[4]

The consumerist vocation ultimately rests on individual performances. The *selection* of services offered by the market which may be needed in order to allow individual performances to run smoothly is also deemed to be the concern of the individual consumer: a task that must be *individually* undertaken and resolved with the help of consumer skills and patterns of action *individually* obtained. Bombarded from all sides by suggestions that they need to equip themselves with one or other shop-supplied product if they want to be able to gain and retain the social standing they desire, perform their social obligations and protect their self-esteem – as well as be seen and recognized as doing all that – consumers of both sexes, all ages and every social standing will feel inadequate, deficient and substandard unless they promptly answer the calls.

For the same reasons (that is, because of the transfer of the issue of 'social fitness' to the responsibility and care of individuals), exclusionist practices in the society of consumers are much stricter, harsher and more unyielding than in the society of producers. In a society of producers, it is males unable to measure up to and pass the test producing/soldiering capacity who are cast as 'abnormal' and branded as 'invalids'; they are subsequently categorized, alternatively, as objects of therapy in the hope of making them fit again and bringing them back 'into the ranks', or of penal policy, to discourage them from resisting a return to the fold. In the society of consumers, the 'invalids' earmarked for exclusion (an ultimate, irrevocable exclusion with no appeal allowed) are 'flawed consumers'. Unlike the misfits of the society of producers (the unemployed and the rejects from military service), they cannot be conceived of as people deserving care and assistance, since following and fulfilling the precepts of consumer culture are presumed (blatantly counterfactually) to be permanently and universally attainable. Being amenable to adoption and application by everyone who so wishes (people may be refused jobs in spite of having the skills it needs, but, unless we speak of a communist 'dictatorship over needs', they can't be refused a consumer commodity if they have the money to pay its price), obeying the precepts is believed (again counterfactually) to depend solely on individual willingness and performance. Because of that assumption, any 'social invalidity' followed by exclusion can, in the society of consumers, only be the outcome of individual faults; any suspicion of 'extrinsic' causes of failure, supra-individual and rooted in society, are eliminated from the start, or at least cast into doubt and disqualified as a valid defence.

'To consume' therefore means to invest in one's own social membership, which in a society of consumers translates as 'saleability': obtaining qualities for which there is already a market demand, or recycling the qualities already possessed into commodities for which demand can go on to be created. Most consumer commodities on offer in the consumer market derive their attraction and their power to enlist keen customers from their genuine or imputed, explicitly advertised or obliquely implied *investment* value. Their promise to increase the attractiveness and consequently the market price of their buyers is written, in a large or small print, or at least between the lines, into the prospectuses of all products – including those products which are, ostensibly, to be purchased mostly or even exclusively for the sake of pure consumer delight; consumption is an investment in everything that matters for individual 'social value' and self-esteem.

The crucial, perhaps the decisive purpose of consumption in the society of consumers (even if it is seldom spelled out in so many words and still less frequently publicly debated) is not the satisfaction of needs, desires and wants, but the commoditization or recommoditization of the consumer: *raising the status of consumers to that of sellable commodities*. It is ultimately for that reason that the passing of the consumer test is a non-negotiable condition of admission to the society that has been reshaped in the likeness of the market-place. The passing of that test is a *non-*contractual precondition of all the *contractual* relations that weave and are woven into the web of relationships called the 'society of consumers'. It is that precondition with no exception allowed and no refusal tolerated which welds the aggregate of seller and buyer transactions into an imagined totality; or which, more exactly, allows that aggregate to be experienced as a totality called 'society' – an entity to which the capacity of 'making demands' and of coercing actors to obey them can be ascribed – allowing the status of a 'social fact' in the Durkheimian sense to be imputed.

Members of the society of consumers are themselves consumer commodities, and it is the quality of being a consumer commodity that makes them bona fide members of that society. Becoming and remaining a sellable commodity is the most potent motive of consumer concerns, even if it is usually latent and seldom conscious, let alone explicitly declared. It is by their potency to increase the consumer's market price that the attractiveness of consumer goods – the current or potential objects of consumers' desire triggering consumer action – tends to be evaluated. 'Making oneself a sellable commodity' is a DIY job, and individual duty. Let us note: *making* oneself, not just *becoming*, is the challenge and the task. The notion that no one is born a fully human creature, that a lot has yet to be done to *become* fully and truly human, is not the invention of the society of consumers – not even of the modern era. But what Günther Anders described in 1956 as 'Promethean shame',[5] the shame of failing in one's duty to make oneself different (presumably better) than one has 'become', is.

In Anders's words, 'Promethean *challenge*' is the 'refusal to owe anything to someone (or something) else, including oneself', whereas 'Promethean *pride*' consists in 'owing everything, including oneself, to oneself'. Obviously, it is oneself, 'one's *own* self', that is the bone of contention, the stake and the main prize in our present-day rendering of the Promethean way of being-in-the-world (or rather, in the contemporary paraphrase/twisting/perversion of the Promethean ambition). Mere 'becoming', as a consequence of the accident of being conceived and born of one's mother, won't do.

That 'merely being' stops well short of the potential perfection of the artifice has been an axiom of the universally binding (even if not universally accepted) worldview since the beginning of modern, enlightened times. Human beings armed with Reason can and should and would improve on Nature – and also *on their own nature*, that 'nature' which caused their appearance-in-the-world and determined the course of their 'becoming'. The Promethean feat, thereby, was no longer the one-off, legendary accomplishment of a demigod, but the mode, or destiny, of human presence-in-the-world as such. The shape of the world – its degree of 'perfection' – was now a matter of human concern and human purposeful action. And so, albeit rather obliquely, was the shape of every individual human, and his or her degree of perfection.

One step more had to be taken, therefore, for the Promethean challenge and pride to give birth to Promethean *shame*. That fateful step, I suggest, was the passage from the society of producers – with its managerial spirit of normative regulation, its division and coordination of labour, its conformity-generating supervision, and its conformity to being supervised – to the society of consumers, with the intermittently compulsive and willing individualization and self-referential character of its concerns, tasks, ways of handling the tasks and responsibilities for the effects of their handling. That step augured a magnified emphasis, dwarfing everything else, on 'oneself' as simultaneously the main *object* and the main *subject* of the duty to remake the world, as well as of the responsibility for its fulfilment or failure: an emphasis on the individual self as at the same time the warden and the ward of the Promethean mode of being.

Bidding openly for its ascendancy over its members, for the priority of 'societal' over individual and 'group' interests and ambitions, and by the same token assuming authorship of the world viewed as an artifice of human action guided by reason, the society of producers assumed, by design or default, the role of a 'collective Prometheus' – thereby substituting conformity to the norm for the individual's responsibility for the quality of the product. The society of consumers 'outsources', 'contracts out', 'subsidiarizes' the Prometheus role, together with responsibility for its performance, to individuals. Promethean shame, unlike Promethean challenge or pride, is a thoroughly individual sentiment. 'Societies' are never ashamed nor can they be shamed; shame is conceivable only as an individual condition.

Having explicitly or at least in practice renounced and discarded the Promethean status it previously claimed, society now hides behind its artifices. The authority and privileges due to a superior being, once the unique and jealously guarded possession of 'human society', has fallen to human products, those material traces of human reason, inventiveness and skill. They are the ones capable of performing perfectly or nearly perfectly the jobs that a 'man born of woman', a mere side-effect of hopelessly contingent nature, would rather botch or at any rate perform in a shamefully inferior manner. It is the artifice, encountered daily in the shape of products of the consumer industry, that now hovers and towers over the head of each and every human individual as the paragon of perfection and the pattern for an effort of emulation (admittedly doomed to fail).

Having accepted the superiority of the *res* (thing), Anders suggests, 'humans reject the incompleteness of their own reification as tantamount to defeat'. Being born and 'having become', instead of being completely fabricated from start to finish, are now a reason to be ashamed. Promethean shame is a sentiment which 'overwhelms men and women at the sight of the humiliatingly high quality of things they themselves fabricated'. Quoting Nietzsche, Anders suggests that nowadays the human body (that is the body as it has been received by the accident of nature) is something that 'must be overcome' and left behind. The 'raw', unadorned, un-re-formed and unprocessed body is something to be ashamed of: offensive to the eye, always leaving much to be desired, and above all a living testimony to a failure of duty, and perhaps to the ineptitude, ignorance, impotence and resourcelessness of 'the self'. The 'naked body', the object which by common consent should not be publicly exposed for reasons of the decorum and dignity of its 'owner', these days does not mean, Anders suggests, 'the body unclothed, but a body on which no work has been done' – an insufficiently 'reified' body.

Being a member of the society of consumers is a daunting task, a never-ending and uphill struggle. The fear of failing to conform has been elbowed out by a fear of inadequacy, but it has not become less haunting for that reason. Consumer markets are eager to capitalize on that fear, and companies turning out consumer goods vie for the status of the most reliable guide and helper in their clients' unending effort to rise to the challenge. They supply 'the tools', the instruments required by the individually performed job of 'self-fabrication'. They could, however, be sued under the Trade Descriptions Act: the goods they make out to be 'tools' for individual use in decision-making are in fact, as Anders insists, 'decisions made in advance'.[6] They were ready-made well before the individual was confronted with the duty (represented as an opportunity) to decide. It is absurd, as Anders says, to think of those tools as enabling an individual choice of purpose. These instruments are the crystallization of irresistible 'necessity' – which, now as before, humans must learn, obey, and learn to obey, in order to be free . . .

Among the sixteen- and seventeen-year-old girls interviewed in the Cotswolds by Decca Aitkenhead, the insightful *Guardian* correspondent, one confessed:

> Well, if I went out in what I'm wearing now (jeans and a T-shirt) people would stare and go, why aren't you wearing some special, sexually provocative clothes? At the age of 13 we were going out dressed like that. That's just what you wear to look fashionable.[7]

Another in the group, who was over twenty, adds that 'the reminders of what a sexy body looks like are everywhere, and as I get older I worry more and more about how I measure up.' The meanings of 'sexually provocative clothes' and the 'look of the sexy body' are both determined by the current fashion (fashion changes, and fast: the sixteen- and seventeen-year-olds 'have no idea that pre-teen T-shorts with slogans such as "Trainee Babe" came into fashion only in the 90s, and seem amazed that girls once dressed differently'; one of them 'looks incredulous', Aitkenhead notices, when told that 'in the 70s girls didn't shave their armpits'). ~~Obtaining new versions of these clothes and grooming these looks and replacing or regrooming the outdated versions are a condition of being and staying in demand: of remaining desirable enough to find willing customers, whether or not money is to be exchanged.~~ As Digby Jones, the outgoing director of the Confederation of British Industry, points out, referring to an altogether different labour market, the sole condition for people wishing to be a 'commodity in demand' is 'to be so adaptable, trained and valuable that no employer would dare to tell them to go or treat them badly'.[8]

In its dominant 'Whig' version (that is, in its 'official transcript', routinely replicated by learned descriptions and popular imaginary alike), the history of humanity is represented as a long march towards personal freedom and rationality.

Its latest stage, the passage from the society of producers and soldiers to the society of consumers, is commonly portrayed as a process of gradual, ultimately to be complete, emancipation of individuals from the original conditions of 'no choice' and later 'limited choice', from pre-scripted scenarios and obligatory routines, from preordained and prescribed, non-negotiable bonds and from compulsory or at least unchallengeable behavioural patterns. In short, that passage is portrayed as another, possibly the conclusive, leap from the world of constraints and unfreedom towards individual autonomy and self-mastery. More often than not, that passage is painted as the final triumph of the individual's right to self-assertion, understood primarily as the indivisible sovereignty of the unencumbered subject; a sovereignty which tends in turn to be interpreted as the individual's right to free choice. The individual member of the society of consumers is defined, first and foremost, as *homo eligens*.

The other, latent transcript, seldom if ever vented in public but always a hidden and invisible, but indispensable prompter of the first, would show the same passage in quite a different light.

Rather than being a step towards the ultimate emancipation of the individual from multiple external coercions, that passage may be shown to be the conquest, annexation and colonization of life by the commodity market – the most profound (even though repressed and concealed) meaning of that conquest and colonization being the elevation of the written and unwritten laws of the market to the rank of life precepts; the kind of precepts that can be ignored only at the rule-breaker's peril, tending to be punished by their exclusion.

Market laws apply, equitably, to the things chosen as much as to their choosers. Only commodities can enter the temples of consumption by right, whether through the 'goods' or the 'clients' entrance; inside those temples, both the objects of worship and their worshippers are commodities. Members of the society of consumers are themselves products of commoditization; their deregulated, privatized relegation to the realm of the commoditization of life politics is the main distinction which sets the society of consumers apart from other forms of human togetherness. As if in a gruesome parody of Kant's categorical imperative, members of the consumer society are obliged to follow the self-same behaviour patterns they wish the objects of their consumption to obey.

To enter the society of consumers and be issued permanent residence permits, men and women must meet the conditions of eligibility defined by market standards. They are expected to make themselves available on the market and to seek, in competition with the rest of the members, their most favourable 'market value'. While exploring the marketplace in search of consumer goods (the ostensible purpose of their presence there), they are drawn to the shops by the prospect of finding the tools and raw materials they may (and *must*) use in making themselves 'fit for being consumed' – and so market-worthy.

Consumption is the principal mechanism of the 'commoditization' of consumers – a task which has been, like so many other socially undertaken and state-managed tasks, deregulated, privatized, 'outsourced' or 'subsidiarized' to consumers and left to the care, administration and responsibility of individual men and women. The driving force of consumer activities is the individual pursuit of the optimal selling price, promotion to a higher division, reaching higher ratings and advancing to a higher position in this or that league table (fortunately, there is a profusion of tables around to watch and hopefully to pick from).

All members of the society of consumers are, from cradle to coffin, consumers *de jure* – even if the *jus* that defined them as consumers has never been voted in by any parliament and has never been recorded in the law books.

Being a 'consumer *de jure*' is for all practical intents and purposes the 'non-legal foundation of the law', since it precedes all legal pronouncements defining and spelling out the entitlements and obligations of the citizen. Courtesy of the groundwork accomplished by the markets, the legislators can take it for granted that the subjects of legislation are already fully fledged, accomplished consumers: wherever it matters, they can treat the condition of being a consumer as a product of nature, not a legal construct – as part of that 'human nature' and inborn human predilection that all positive laws are obliged to respect, attend to, obey, protect and service; indeed, as that primordial *human* right underlying all *citizen* rights, the kinds of secondary rights whose major task is to reconfirm that basic, primary right as sacrosanct, and render it fully and truly unassailable.

Having studied and reconstructed the sequence of developments following the First World War, the developments which led eventually to the entrenchment of the society of consumers, Daniel Thomas Cook concluded that

> children's 'right' to consume in many ways precedes and prefigures other, legally constituted rights. Children had been given a 'voice' on the retail sales floor, in 'design-it and name-it' contests, in clothing choice, and in marketers' research designs decades before their rights were asserted in such contexts as the UN Convention on the Rights of the Child in 1989. Children's participation in the world of goods as actors, as persons with desire, underpins their current, emergent status as right-bearing individuals.[9]

While focusing on the history of children's consumerism and the twentieth century's commoditization of childhood (or, to use the terms he coined, the 'Copernican revolution' accomplished by markets targeted on children and consisting of the switch from the 'parents perspective' to 'pediocularity', that is the adjustment of designing and marketing strategies to the point of view of the child, now recognized as a sovereign subject of desires and choice-making), Cook came across a universal pattern followed by the society of consumers in its original development and still followed in its self-reproduction and expansion. One is tempted to redeploy in the analysis of the production of consumers and the reproduction of the society of consumers the memorable suggestion made by Ernst Haeckel, the notorious and celebrated nineteenth-century naturalist, that 'ontogenesis is a recapitulation of philogenesis' (meaning that the stages of development of an individual embryo are abbreviated and compressed recapitulations of the stages passed through by the species in its historical evolution), though with one crucial proviso: instead of implying a one-directional causality, it is reasonable and proper to propose (in order to prevent the notoriously idle, since unresolvable, debate of the 'which came first, the chicken or the egg' variety) that the same sequence is imposed on to the life-path of the individual consumer as tends to be endlessly repeated in the ongoing reproduction of the society of consumers.

In the daily operation of the present-day, mature society of consumers, the 'rights of the child' *and* the 'rights of the citizen' are grounded in, and overlie, the genuine or assumed capacity of the competent consumer – just as they did during its emergence and maturation. The two sequences mutually reassert and reinforce, 'naturalizing' each other and helping each other into the status of 'dominant ideas' – but more to the point into the treasury of *doxa* (assumptions people think with though seldom if ever about) or, purely and simply, of common sense.

In opposition to the *formal right*, in the awarding of which any 'means testing' is, again, *formally* disallowed, the condition – seldom spelled out frankly and yet decisive – of awarding or refusing the practical, *substantive* entitlement to the benefits of fully fledged citizenship is a person's consumerist competence and the ability to use it. A considerable number of consumers *de jure* fail the test which has been set, informally yet all too tangibly, for consumers *de facto*. These who fail the test are 'failed consumers', sometimes subcategorized as 'failed asylum seekers' or 'unlawful immigrants', at other times as the 'underclass' (that is, a motley assortment of individuals refused access to any of the acknowledged social classes, ineligible for class membership as such), but most of the time scattered anonymously in the statistics of the 'poor' or 'people below the poverty line' – according to Simmel's classic definition the objects of charity, rather than discerning/ choosing subjects like the rest of the members of the society of consumers. If one agrees with Carl Schmitt's proposition that the ultimate, defining prerogative of sovereign is the right to exempt, then one must accept that the *true carrier of sovereign power in the society of consumers is the commodity market*; it is there, at the meeting place of sellers and buyers, that selecting and setting apart the damned from the saved, insiders from outsiders, the included from the excluded (or, more to the point, right-and-proper consumers from flawed ones) is daily performed.

The consumer commodity market, one has to admit, makes a peculiar, bizarre sovereign, starkly distinct from those familiar to the readers of political science tracts. This strange sovereign has neither legislative nor executive agencies, not to mention courts of law – which are rightly viewed as the indispensable paraphernalia of the bona fide sovereigns explored and described in political science textbooks. In consequence, the market is, so to speak, more sovereign than the much more advertised and eagerly self-advertising political sovereigns, since in addition to returning the verdicts of exclusion, the market allows for no appeals procedure. Its sentences are as firm and irrevocable as they are informal, tacit and seldom if ever spelled out in writing. Exemption by the organs of a sovereign state can be objected to and protested against, and so stands a chance of being annulled – but not eviction by the sovereign market, because no presiding judge is named here, no receptionist is in sight to accept appeal papers, while no address has been given to which they could be mailed.

For disallowing the protestations that may follow the verdicts of the market, politicians have the tested formula of TINA ('There is no alternative') – a diagnosis all but self-fulfilling, a hypothesis all but self-confirming. The more often the formula is repeated, the more thorough is the surrender of the state's sovereignty over the consumer commodity markets and the more redoubtable and intractable the sovereignty of the markets becomes.

As a matter of fact, it is not the *state*, not even its executive arm, that is being sapped, eroded, emaciated, or is otherwise 'withering away' – but the state's *sovereignty*, its prerogative to draw the line between the included and the excluded, complete with the right to rehabilitate and readmit the latter.

Partly, that sovereignty has been already somewhat limited, and we can guess that under the pressure of the emergence of globally binding laws supported by juridical organs (partial and rudimentary thus far), it will probably continue, in fits and starts, to shrink. This process is of only secondary and derivative relevance to the issue of the new sovereignty of markets, however, changing little in the way sovereign decisions are taken and legitimated. Even if it is moved 'higher up', to suprastate institutions, sovereignty (at least in the principle it is supposed or deemed to fulfil) still blends power with politics and subordinates the first to the supervision of the second; most importantly, it may be contested and reformed thanks to having a fixed address.

Much more revolutionary (and potentially fatal to the state as it was shaped during the modern era) is another tendency, undermining the state's sovereignty much more thoroughly: the inclination of the weakened state to move many of its functions and prerogatives sideways rather than upwards, ceding them to the impersonal powers of markets; or the ever more comprehensive surrender of the state to the blackmail of market forces counteracting the policies favoured and endorsed by its electorate and taking over from the citizenship the status of the reference point and ultimate arbiter of political propriety.

The result of this second tendency is the gradual separation between the *power to act*, which now drifts towards the markets, and *politics*, which, though remaining the domain of the state, is progressively stripped of its freedom of manoeuvre and power to set the rules and be arbiter of the game. This is indeed the prime cause of the erosion of the state's sovereignty. Though state organs continue to articulate, spell out and execute the sentences of exemption or eviction, they are no longer free to decide the criteria of the 'policy of exemption' or the principles of its application. The state as a whole, including its legislative and juridical arms, becomes an executor of market sovereignty.

When a minister of the government declares, for instance, that the new immigration policy will be aimed at bringing into Britain more people 'whom the country needs' and at keeping out those 'for whom the country has no need', he implicitly gives to the markets the right to define the 'needs of the country' and to decide what (or whom) the country needs and what (or whom) it does not need. What the minister therefore has in mind is to offer hospitality to people who promise to be or soon become exemplary consumers, while withholding it from people whose patterns of consumption – characteristic of people at the bottom of the income ladder, of people who focus on the less profitable or unprofitable consumer goods – will not prompt the wheels of the consumer economy to rotate faster than they do and boost company profits above the levels already achieved. As if to emphasize further the principles guiding the thinking and reasoning behind the approval or disapproval of foreigners, the minister points out that the income earned by those few people in the latter category who may be temporarily admitted to meet the seasonal needs of necessarily local consumer production (hotel and restaurant services, or fruit picking) will be transferred to their countries of origin (since members of their families won't be allowed to follow them into Britain), and so will not invigorate the circulation of consumer goods inside the country. The flawed consumers, people in command of too few resources to respond adequately to the 'hailing', or more exactly the seductive passes of the commodity markets, are people the society of consumers 'does not need'; the society of consumers would be better off without them. In a society that measures its success and failure by GNP statistics (that is, by the sum total of money that changes hands in buying and selling transactions), such impaired, defective consumers are written off as liabilities.

The tacit assumption underlying all that reasoning is again the formula of 'no consumer unless a commodity'. Commoditization precedes consumption and controls the entry into the world of consumers. One needs to become a commodity first to stand a reasonable chance of exercising the rights and fulfilling the duties of a consumer. 'The country', like the markets, needs commodities; a country which surrenders to the consumer markets the right of first and last say needs residents who either are commodities already or are amenable to swift and inexpensive commoditization; assignment to the category of bona fide commodity is, of course, a matter for the markets to decide. 'Are there buyers for this particular variety of goods?' is the first and final question to be asked whenever an application to enter and stay in the country is being pondered by state officials.

The government took over and reforged into a principle of state policy the pattern and rule already established and entrenched in the daily life of consumerist society by the widespread practices of the liquid modern enterprise. As Nicole Aubert found in her thorough study of such practices, the personnel policies of big capitalist enterprises are conducted 'as if the employees were themselves "products", having been conceived, used and renewed in the shortest possible time'.[10] Those newly recruited are expected to perform at full speed and strength from the first day of their employment: there is no time for 'settling down', becoming 'rooted', integrating and developing loyalty to the company and solidarity with its other employees, since the profile of the services required changes too fast to leave time for adjustment. Lengthy recruitment processes, adjustment and in-company training are all seen as a waste of time and resources – like keeping excessive stocks of finished products in the company's warehouses; when they are lying on shelves, the products bring no profit and are for all practical purposes useless. Both the stocks and time for recruitment, integration and training need to be reduced to the bare minimum.

The secret of every durable (that is, successfully self-reproducing) social system is the recasting of its 'functional prerequisites' into behavioural motives of actors.

To put it a different way, the secret of all successful 'socialization' is making individuals *wish to do* what *is needed* to enable the system to reproduce itself. This may be done openly and *explicitly*, mustering and beefing up support for the declared interests of a 'whole', like a state or a nation, through a process variously dubbed 'spiritual mobilization', 'civic education' or 'ideological indoctrination', as it was usually done in the 'solid' phase of modernity, in the 'society of producers'. Or it may be done surreptitiously and *obliquely*, through overtly or covertly enforcing or drilling in certain behavioural patterns, as well as certain patterns of problem-solving, which – once embraced and observed (as observed they must be, because alternative choices recede and vanish, with a gradual yet relentless forgetting of the skills needed to practise them) – will sustain the monotonous reproduction of the system – as it is usually done in the 'liquid' phase of modernity that happens to be also the time of the society of consumers.

That way of tying together the 'systemic prerequisites' and the individual motives typical of the society of producers required a devaluation of the 'now', and particularly of immediate satisfaction and more generally of enjoyment (or rather of what the French mean by the virtually untranslatable concept of *jouissance*). The 'present' had to be demoted to the role of second fiddle to the 'future', thereby giving away its meaning as a hostage to the as yet undisclosed turns of a history believed to be tamed, conquered and controlled precisely through knowledge of its laws and surrender to their demands. The 'present' was just a means to an end, that is to a happiness that was always in the future, always 'not yet'.

By the same token, that way of coordinating systemic prerequisites with individual motives had necessarily also to promote procrastination, and in particular to enthrone the precept of 'delaying' or surrendering 'gratification' – that is, the precept of sacrificing quite specific, immediately available rewards in the name of imprecise future benefits; as well as sacrificing individual rewards for the benefit of the 'whole' (be it society, state, nation, class, gender or just a deliberately underspecified 'we'), trusting that it would in due course secure a better life for all. In a society of producers, the 'long term' was given preference over the 'short term', and the needs of the 'whole' were given priority over the needs of its 'parts'. The joys and satisfaction derived from 'eternal' and 'supra-individual' values were cast as superior to fleeting individual raptures, while the raptures of the greater number were put above the plight of the fewer – regarded as the only genuine and worthy satisfactions amidst the multitude of seductive but false, contrived, deceptive and ultimately degrading 'pleasures of the moment'.

Wise after the event, we (men and women whose lives are conducted in the liquid modern setting) are more often than not inclined to dismiss that way of dovetailing systemic reproduction with individual motivations as wasteful, exorbitantly costly and, above all, abominably oppressive – since it goes against the grain of 'natural' human proclivities. Sigmund Freud was one of the first thinkers to note that – though even that exquisitely imaginative thinker, gathering his data as he had to from a life lived on the rising slope of the society of mass industry and mass conscription, was unable to conceive of an alternative to the coercive suppression of instincts, and so ascribed to what he observed the generic status of necessary and unavoidable features of all and any civilization: civilization 'as such'.[11]

Nowhere and under no circumstances, Freud concluded, will the demand of instinct renunciation be willingly embraced. A substantive majority of humans obey many of the necessary cultural prohibitions or precepts 'only under the pressure of external coercion'. 'It is alarming to think of the enormous amount of coercion that will inevitably be required' to promote, instil and make safe the necessary civilizing choices, such as, for instance, the work ethic (that is, a wholesale condemnation of leisure coupled with the commandment to work for work's sake whatever the material rewards), or the ethic of peaceful cohabitation proposed by the commandment 'Thou shalt love thy neighbour as thyself' ('What is the point of a precept enunciated with so much solemnity,' Freud asks rhetorically, 'if its fulfilment cannot be recommended as reasonable?').

The rest of Freud's case for the coercive scaffolding all civilizations need to remain upright is too well known to be restated here in any detail. The overall conclusion, as we know, was that all and any civilization must be sustained by repression, since some amount of constantly simmering dissent and sporadic yet repetitive rebellion, as well as a continuous effort to hold them down or pre-empt them, are unavoidable. Disaffection and mutiny cannot be avoided, since all civilization means the repressive containment of human instincts and all constraint is repulsive.

> (T)he replacement of the power of the individual by the power of community constitutes the decisive step of civilization. The essence of it lies in the fact that the members of the community restrict themselves in their possibilities of satisfaction, whereas the individual knew no such restriction.

Let's leave aside the caveat that 'the individual' who is not always already a 'member of a community' may be a yet more mythical figure than Hobbes's pre-social savage of the *bellum omnium contra omnes* (war of all against all), or be just a rhetorical device for the sake of the argument, like the 'original patricide' that Freud would invent in his later work. However, whatever the reason why the particular wording of the message was chosen, the substance of the message is that since the hoi-polloi are unlikely willingly to acknowledge, embrace and obey the commandment of putting the interests of a supra-individual group above individual inclinations and impulses, and of placing long-term effects above immediate satisfactions (as in the case of the work ethic), any civilization (or, to put it more simply, any kind of human peaceful and cooperative cohabitation with all its benefits) *must* rest on coercion, or at least on a realistic threat that coercion will be applied if the restrictions imposed on instinctual impulses are not punctiliously observed. By hook or by crook, the 'reality principle' must be assured an upper hand over the 'pleasure principle' if civilized human togetherness is to persist. Freud re-projects this conclusion on all types of human togetherness (retrospectively renamed 'civilizations'), presenting it as a *universal* precondition of human togetherness; of *all* life-in-society, which admittedly is coterminous with *human* life as such.

But whatever answer is given to the question of whether or not the repression of instincts was indeed, and will forever remain, coterminous with the history of humanity, one can credibly suggest that this apparently timeless principle could not have been discovered, named, put on record or theorized at any other time than at the dawn of the modern era; more to the point, at no other time than just after the disintegration of the *ancien régime* that immediately preceded it. It was that disintegration, the falling apart of the customary institutions that had sustained a by and large monotonous and more or less matter of fact reproduction of *Rechts-* and *Pflichts-Gewohnenheiten* (customary rights and duties), that laid bare the human-made artifice hiding behind the idea of the 'natural' or 'Divine' order, and so forced a reclassification of the phenomenon of order from the category of the 'given' to the category of 'tasks', thus re-representing the '*logic* of *Divine* creation' as an *achievement* of *human* power.

And yet the point is, though, that even if room for coercion before the advent of the modern era was no less ample than it was bound to become in the course of building the modern order (and it was), there was hardly room there for the self-assurance and matter-of-factness with which Jeremy Bentham could and did put an equation mark between obedience to law on the one side, and making sure that no alternative choices could seep in, on the other – through locking the exits from panoptical confinement

while putting the inmates into a situation where their choice was
'work or die'. Richard Rorty summed up the trend in one short,
pithy proposition: 'With Hegel, the intellectuals began to switch
over from fantasies of contacting eternity to fantasies of constructing a better future.'[12]

The 'power of community', and particularly of an artificially
built community, a community brought into being in the course
of building a civilization or a nation, did not have to *replace* 'the
power of the individual' to make cohabitation feasible and viable;
the power of community was in place long *before* its necessity, let
alone its urgency, was discovered. Indeed, the idea that such a
replacement was a task still to be performed by a powerful agent,
collective or individual, was unlikely to occur to either 'the individual' or 'the community' as long as the presence of community
and its all-too-tangible power was, so to speak, 'hiding in the
light': *too evident to be noticed.* The community, as it were, held
power over the individual (and a total, 'everything included' kind
of power) as long as it remained *unproblematical*, and not a *task*
that (like all tasks) could be fulfilled *or* fail to be fulfilled. To put
it in a nutshell, the community held individuals in its grip as long
as they lived in ignorance of 'being a community'.

Turning the subordination of individual powers to those of a
'community' into a 'need' waiting 'to be met', and calling for
measures to be deliberately undertaken, reversed the logic of premodern social forms; though at the same time, by 'naturalizing'
what was in fact a historical process, it generated in one fell swoop
its own legitimacy and the etiological myth of its 'origin', 'birth'
or 'creation'; of an act or process of recasting, integrating and
condensing an aggregate of free-floating, solitary and mutually
suspicious and hostile individuals into a 'community' able to bid
successfully for the authority to trim and repress such individual
predispositions as were revealed or declared to be contrary to the
requirements of secure cohabitation.

To cut a long story short, *community* might be as old as
humanity, but the *idea* of 'community' as a condition *sine qua
non* of humanity could be born only together with the experience
of its crisis. That idea was patched out of the fears emanating
from the disintegration of the earlier self-reproducing social settings – called subsequently, and retrospectively, the *ancien régime*,
and recorded in the social-scientific vocabulary under the name

of the 'traditional society'. The *modern* 'civilizing process' (the *only* process calling itself by that name) was triggered by the state of uncertainty, for which the falling apart and impotence of 'community' was one of the suggested explanations.

The 'nation', that eminently modern innovation, was visualized in the likeness of 'community': it was to be a new and bigger community, community writ large, community projected on the large screen of a newly imagined 'totality' – and a community-by-design, a community made to the measure of the newly extended network of human interdependencies and exchanges. What was given the name of the 'civilizing process' later, at a time when the developments to which it referred were already fast grinding to a halt or apparently going into reverse, was a steady attempt to reregularize or repattern human conduct once it was no longer subjected to the homogenizing pressures of self-reproducing pre-modern neighbourhoods.

Ostensibly, the process retrospectively dubbed 'civilizing' was focused on individuals: the new capacity of self-control by the newly autonomous *individual* was to take over the job done before by the *communal* controls no longer available. But the genuine stake of the bid was the deployment of the self-controlling capacity of the individuals in the service of re-enacting or reconstituting 'community' at a higher level. Just as the ghost of the lost Roman Empire hovered over the self-constitution of feudal Europe, the ghost of lost community soared over the constitution of modern nations. Nation-building was to be accomplished while using patriotism – an induced (taught and learned) readiness to sacrifice individual interests to the interests shared with other individuals ready to do the same – as its principal raw material. As Ernest Renan famously summed up that strategy: nation was, or rather could only live and survive by, the daily plebiscite of its members.

Setting about restoring historicity to Freud's timeless model of civilization, Norbert Elias explained the birth of the modern self (that awareness of one's own 'inner truth', coupled with one's own responsibility for its self-assertion) by the internalization of external constraints and their pressures. The nation-building process was inscribed in the space extending between supra-individual panoptical powers and the individual capacity to accommodate to the necessities which those powers set in place. The newly acquired individual *freedom of choice* (including the choice of self-identity) resulting from the unprecedented underdetermination and underdefinition of social placement, caused in turn by the demise or radical weakening of traditional bonds, was to be deployed, paradoxically, in the service of the *suppression of choices* deemed detrimental to the 'new totality': the community-like nation-state.

Whatever its pragmatic merits might be, the Panopticon-style 'discipline, punish and rule' way of achieving the needed and intended manipulation and subsequent routinization of behavioural probabilities was cumbersome, costly and conflict-ridden. It was also inconvenient, surely not the best choice for the holders of power since it imposed severe and non-negotiable constraints on their own freedom of manoeuvre. It was not, however, the sole strategy through which the systemic stability better known under the name of 'social order' could be achieved and made secure.

Having identified 'civilization' with a centralized system of coercion and indoctrination (later all but reducing it, under Michel Foucault's influence, to its coercive wing), social scientists were left with little choice except to describe, misleadingly, the advent of the 'postmodern condition' (a development coinciding with the entrenchment of the society of consumers) as a product of the 'de-civilizing process'. What in fact happened, though, was the discovery, invention or emergence of an alternative method (less cumbersome, less costly and relatively less conflict-ridden, but above all giving more freedom, and so more power, to the power-holders) of manipulating the behavioural probabilities necessary to sustain the system of domination recognized as social order. Another variety of the 'civilizing process', an alternative and apparently more convenient way in which the task of that process could be pursued, was found and set in place.

This new way, practised by the liquid modern society of consumers, arouses little if any dissent, resistance or rebellion thanks to the expedient of representing the new *obligation* (the obligation to choose) as *freedom* of choice. One could say that the much pondered, criticized and reviled oracle of Jean-Jacques Rousseau – that 'people must be forced to be free' – came true, after centuries, though not in the form in which both the ardent followers and the severe critics of Rousseau expected it to be implemented . . .

One way or another, the opposition between the 'pleasure' and the 'reality' principles, until recently deemed to be implacable, has been overridden: surrendering to the stern demands of the 'reality principle' translates as fulfilment of the obligation to seek pleasure and happiness, so it is lived through as an exercise of freedom and an act of self-assertion. One is tempted to say that Hegel's admittedly controversial formula of freedom as 'necessity understood' has become self-fulfilling – though, ironically, only thanks to a mechanism capable of leaving the 'understanding' bit out of recycling the pressures of necessity into an experience of freedom. Punishing force, if applied, is seldom naked; it comes disguised as the result of one or other 'false step', or of this or that lost (overlooked) opportunity. Far from revealing the hidden limits of individual freedom and bringing them into the light, it hides them yet more securely by obliquely retrenching the individual choice (whether already made or yet to be made) in its role of the main, perhaps even the only, 'difference that makes a difference' in the individual pursuit of happiness – between effective and ineffective steps, between victory and defeat.

More often than not, the 'totality' to which individuals are to stay loyal and obedient no longer enters their life and confronts them in the shape of a denial of their individual autonomy, or as an obligatory sacrifice like universal conscription and the duty to give their life for the country and the national cause. Instead, it presents itself in the form of highly entertaining and invariably pleasurable and relished festivals of communal togetherness and belonging, held on the occasions of a football world cup or a cricket test match. Surrender to the 'totality' is no longer a reluctantly embraced, cumbersome and quite often onerous duty, but 'patriotainment', an avidly sought and eminently enjoyable festive revelry.

Carnivals, as Mikhail Bakhtin memorably suggested, tend to be interruptions to the daily routine, brief exhilarating intervals between successive instalments of dull quotidianity, pauses in which the mundane hierarchy of values is temporarily reversed, the most harrowing aspects of reality are briefly suspended, and the kinds of conduct prohibited and considered shameful in 'normal' life are ostentatiously practised and openly brandished.

The old-style carnivals gave a chance for the individual liberties denied in daily life to be ecstatically tasted; now the sorely missed opportunities are those of loosing the burden and burying the anguish of individuality through dissolving the self in a 'greater whole' and joyously abandoning oneself to its rule, celebrating in brief yet intense festivals of communal merry-making. The function (and seductive power) of liquid modern carnivals lies in the momentary resuscitation of the togetherness that has sunk into a coma. Such carnivals are séances for people to gather together to hold hands and call back the ghost of deceased community from the netherworld, for as long as the séance lasts, – safe in their awareness that the guest won't outstay its invitation, will pay but a fleeting visit and promptly vanish again the moment the séance is over.

All that does not mean that the 'normal' weekday conduct of individuals has become random, unpatterned and uncoordinated. It only means that the non-randomness, regularity and coordination of individually undertaken actions can be, and as a rule are, attained by other means than the solid modern contraptions of enforcement, than policing and a chain of command applied by a totality bidding to be 'greater than the sum of its parts' and bent on training and drilling discipline into its 'human units'.

In a liquid modern society of consumers, the *swarm* tends to replace the *group* – with its leaders, hierarchy of authority and pecking order. A swarm can do without all those trappings and stratagems without which a group would neither be formed nor be able to survive. Swarms need not be burdened by the tools of survival; they assemble, disperse and gather again, from one occasion to another, each time guided by different, invariably shifting relevancies, and attracted by changing and moving targets. The seductive power of shifting targets is as a rule sufficient to coordinate their movements, so that any command or other enforcement 'from the top' is made redundant. As a matter of fact, swarms do not have 'tops'; it is solely the current direction of their flight that casts some of the units of the self-propelled swarm into the position of 'leaders' being 'followed' – for the duration of a particular flight or a part of it, though hardly for longer.

Swarms are not teams; they know nothing of the division of labour. They are (unlike bona fide groups) no more than the 'sum of their parts', or rather aggregates of self-propelled units, united solely (to continue revisiting and revising Durkheim) by 'mechanical solidarity', manifested in the replication of similar patterns of conduct and by moving in a similar direction. They can be visualized best as Warhol's endlessly copied images with no original, or with an original discarded after use and impossible to trace and retrieve. Each unit of the swarm re-enacts the moves made by any other, while performing the whole of the job alone, from beginning to end and in all its parts (in the case of consuming swarms, the job so performed is the job of consuming).

In a swarm there are no specialists, no holders of separate (and scarce) skills and resources whose task it is to enable and assist other units to complete their jobs, or to compensate for their individual shortcomings or incapacities. Each unit is a 'Jack of all trades', and needs the complete set of tools and skills necessary for the entire job to be fulfilled. In a swarm there is no exchange, no cooperation, no complementariness – just the physical proximity and roughly coordinated direction of the current movement. In the case of human feeling and thinking units, the comfort of flying in a swarm derives from having security in *numbers*: a belief that the direction of flight must have been properly chosen since an impressively large swarm is following it, a supposition that so many feeling, thinking and freely choosing human beings couldn't be simultaneously fooled. As self-assurance and the sentiment of security go, the miraculously coordinated movements of a swarm are the next best substitute for the authority of group leaders, and no less effective.

Swarms, unlike groups, know nothing of dissenters or rebels – only, so to speak, of 'deserters', 'blunderers' or 'maverick sheep'. Units falling out of the main body in flight have just 'strayed', been 'lost' or have 'fallen by the wayside'. They are bound to forage on their own, but the lives of solitary mavericks will seldom last long, because the chance of finding a realistic target by themselves is much smaller than if they follow a swarm, and when fanciful, useless or dangerous targets are pursued, the risks of perishing multiply.

The society of consumers tends to break up groups or make them eminently fragile and fissiparous, favouring instead the prompt and swift formation and scattering of swarms.

Consumption is a supremely solitary activity (perhaps even the archetype of solitude), even when it happens to be conducted in company.

No lasting bonds emerge in the activity of consumption. Those bonds that manage to be tied in the act of consumption may, but may not, outlast the act; they may hold swarms together for the duration of their flight (that is, until the next change of target), but they are admittedly occasion-bound and otherwise thin and flimsy, having little bearing, if any at all on the subsequent moves of the units, while throwing little if any light on the units' past histories.

Wise after the event, we can surmise that what kept household members round family tables, and made the family table into an instrument of the integration and reassertion of the family as a durably bonded group, was in no small measure the *productive* element in consumption. Food ready to eat could be found at the family table but nowhere else: the gathering at the common dinner table was the last (distributive) stage of a lengthy productive process that started in the kitchen and even beyond, in the family field or workshop. What bonded the diners into a group was the cooperation, accomplished or expected, in the preceding process of productive labour, and sharing consumption of what was produced was derived from that. We may suppose that the 'unintended consequence' of 'fast food', 'take-aways' or 'TV dinners' (or perhaps rather their 'latent function', and the true cause of their unstoppable rise in popularity) is either to make the gatherings around the family table redundant, so putting an end to the shared consumption, or to symbolically endorse the loss, by an act of commensality, consuming in company, of the onerous bond-tying and bond-reaffirming characteristics it once had but which have become irrelevant or even undesirable in the liquid modern society of consumers. 'Fast food' is there to protect the solitude of lone consumers.

Active participation in consumer markets is the main virtue expected of the members of a consumer society (or as the Home Secretary would prefer to put it, of those people 'whom the country needs'). After all, when the 'growth' measured by GNP threatens to slow down, or even more when it might fall below zero, it is consumers reaching for their cheque books, or better still their credit cards, who are hoped, and cajoled and nudged, to 'get the economy going' – in order to 'lead the country out of depression'.

Such hopes and appeals only make sense, of course, if they are addressed to people with bank accounts in the black and a wallet-full of credit cards, to 'credit-worthy' people whom 'listening banks' will listen to, 'smiling banks' smile at and 'banks that like saying "yes"' say yes to. Not surprisingly, the task of making members of the society credit-worthy and willing to use the credit they have been offered to the limit is steadily moving to the top of the list of patriotic duties and efforts at socialization. In Britain, living on credit and in debt has by now become part of the national curriculum, designed, endorsed and subsidized by the government. Students in higher education, the hoped-for 'consumer elite' of the future and so the part of the nation promising the most benefits to the consumer economy in the years to come, undergo three to six years of training, compulsory in all but name, in the skills and usages of borrowing money and living on credit. It is hoped that the obligatory life on loans will last long enough to become a habit, wiping out from the institution of consumer credit any last lingering vestiges of opprobrium (carried over from the savings-book society of producers); and long enough for the belief that debt never repaid is a smart and sound life strategy to be raised to the rank of a 'rational choice' and 'good sense', and to make it into an axiom of life wisdom that is no longer questionable. Indeed, sufficiently long to recycle 'living on credit' into second nature.

This 'second nature' may follow quickly on the heels of the government-sponsored training; immunity to 'natural disasters' and other 'blows of fate' might not, however, come with it. To the wide acclaim of marketers and politicians alike, young men and women will have joined the ranks of 'serious consumers' well before they start to earn their own living, since a twenty-year-old can now obtain a set of credit cards without the slightest difficulty (and no wonder, considering that the challenge of becoming a valued commodity, a task requiring money and ever more money, is a preliminary condition of being admitted to the 'job market'). But recent research conducted under the joint auspices of the Financial Services Authority and Bristol University found that the generation from eighteen to forty years old (that is, the first adult generation brought up and maturing within a fully developed consumer society) is unable to cope with their debts or accumulate anything above an 'alarmingly low' level of savings: only 30 per cent of individuals in that generation have put aside some money for future purchases, while 42 per cent have done nothing to secure any pension prospects, and 24 per cent of the young (though only 11 per cent of the over-fifties and 6 per cent of the over-sixties) are currently overdrawn in their bank accounts.[13]

That living on credit, in debt and with no savings is a right and proper method of running human affairs at all levels, at the level of individual life politics as much as at the level of state politics, has been, so to speak, 'made official' – on the authority of the most successful and most mature among present-day societies of consumers. The United States of America, ostensibly the world's most powerful economy, looked up to as a success model to follow by most inhabitants of the globe who seek the ultimate example of a gratifying and enjoyable life, is perhaps deeper in debt than any other country in history. Paul Krugman points out that 'last year America spent 57 percent more than it earned on world markets', asks 'how did Americans manage to live so far beyond their means?', and answers: 'by running up debts to Japan, China and Middle Eastern oil producers'.[14] The rulers and the citizens of the United States of America are addicted to (and dependent on) imported money as much as they are addicted to and dependent on imported oil. The federal budget deficit of 300 billion dollars was recently hailed by the White House as something to be proud of just because it had cut a few billion from the hundreds of billions of last year's deficit (a calculation, by the way, most likely to be proved false before the budget year is out). State borrowing, just like consumer debt, is meant to finance consumption, not investment. The imported money that will need to be repaid sooner or later (even if the current administration leans over backwards to postpone the repayment *ad calendas graecas*) is not spent on financing potentially profitable investments, but on sustaining the consumer boom and so the 'feel-good factor' in the electorate, and on financing growing federal deficits regularly exacerbated as they are (despite ever more severe cuts in social provision) by continuing tax cuts for the rich.

'Tax cuts for the rich' are not – at any rate not only – recipes for making the great and mighty happier, or for repaying the debts incurred by politicians in the heat of exorbitantly costly electoral battles. It is not enough either to explain the tax-cutting policies by the congenital inclinations of politicians who come mostly from the ranks of the rich (as in probably the most notorious case, also the most widely publicized, though to no avail, of Vice-President Cheney's patronage of the Haliburton company over which he presided before running for federal office and whose management he might be hoping to resume once his term of office ends), or by the corruptibility of those politicians coming from the lower strata who couldn't withstand the temptation to recycle their *political* success, temporary by its nature, into more lasting and reliable *economic* assets.

In addition to all those factors, which have certainly played their part in generating and sustaining the present tendency, cutting the taxes of the rich is an integral part of the overall trend to shift taxation away from *income*, its 'natural' base in the society of producers, to *spending* – a similarly 'natural' base in a society of the consumers. It is now the activity of the consumer, not the producer, which is presumed to provide the essential interface between individuals and the society at large; it is now primarily the capacity of the consumer, not of the producer, which defines the status of the citizen. It is therefore right and proper, in substance as much as symbolically, to refocus the interplay of rights and duty, routinely evoked to legitimize charging and collecting tax, on the sovereign choices of the consumer.

Unlike income tax, value added tax, or VAT, brings into focus that freedom of (consumer) choice which in the common sense of the society of consumers defines the meaning of individual sovereignty and human rights, and which governments presiding over societies of consumers brandish and flaunt as the kind of service whose delivery supplies all the legitimacy their power needs.

3

Consumerist Culture

An influential, widely read and respected fashion handbook, edited by a highly prestigious journal for the autumn–winter 2005 season, offered 'half a dozen key looks' 'for the coming months' 'that will put you ahead of the style pack'. This promise was aptly, skilfully calculated to catch the attention: and very skilfully indeed, since in a brief, crisp sentence it managed to address all or almost all anxious concerns and urges bred by the society of consumers and born of consuming life.

First, the concern 'to be and to stay ahead' (ahead of the 'style pack' – that is, of the reference group, of the 'significant others', the 'others who count' and whose approval or rejection draws the line between success and failure). In the words of Michel Maffesoli, 'I am who I am because others recognize me as such', while 'the empirical social life is but an expression of sentiments of successive belongings'[1] – the alternative being a succession of rejections or an ultimate exclusion, as a penalty for the failure to force, argue or wriggle one's way into recognition.

It needs to be remembered, though, that in a society of consumers, where human bonds tend to lead through and be mediated by the markets for consumer goods, the sentiment of belonging is not obtained by following the procedure administered and supervised by those 'style packs' to which one aspires, but through the aspirant's own metonymical identification with the 'pack'; the process of self-identification is pursued, and its results are displayed, with the help of visible 'marks of belonging', obtainable as a rule in the shops. In the 'postmodern tribes' (as Maffesoli prefers to call the 'style packs' of consumer society), 'emblematic figures' and their visible marks (clues suggestive of dress and/or conduct codes) replace the 'totems' of the original tribes. *Being* ahead in sporting the emblems of the style pack's emblematic figures is the sole trustworthy prescription for gaining the conviction that if it was aware of the aspirant's existence the style pack of one's choice would indeed accord the desired recognition and acceptance; while *staying* ahead is the only way to make such an acknowledgment of 'belonging' secure for the desired duration – that is, to solidify the single act of admission into a (fixed-time, albeit renewable) residence permit. All in all, 'being ahead' augurs a chance of security, certainty and the certainty of security – precisely the kinds of experience which the consuming life most conspicuously and painfully misses, in spite of being guided by the desire to acquire it.

The reference to '*being* ahead of the style pack' conveys the promise of a high market value and a profusion of demand (both translated as a certainty of recognition, approval and inclusion). In the case of a bid reduced by and large to the display of emblems, a bid that starts from the purchase of emblems, goes through a public announcement of their possession and is seen as completed once possession becomes public knowledge, this translates in turn into the sentiment of 'belonging'. The reference to '*staying* ahead' intuits a reliable precaution against the danger of overlooking the moment when the current emblems of 'belonging' go out of circulation, having been replaced by fresh ones, and when their inattentive bearers risk falling by the wayside – which, in the case of the market-mediated bid for membership, translates as the sentiment of being rejected, excluded, abandoned and lonely, and ultimately rebounds in the searing pain of personal inadequacy. Unpacking the hidden meaning of consumer (consuming) concerns, Mary Douglas famously suggested that a theory of needs 'should start by assuming that any individual needs goods in order to commit other people to his projects . . . Goods are for mobilizing other people.'[2] Or at least for the comforting feeling that all that needed to be done to achieve such mobilization, has been.

Second, the message comes with a use-by date: readers be warned – it holds 'for the coming months' and no longer. It chimes well with the experience of pointillist time composed of instants, of fixed-term episodes and new starts; it liberates the present, which is to be explored and exploited in full, from the distractions of the past and the future that might have impeached the concentration and spoiled the exhilaration of free choice. It offers a double bonus of being momentarily up-to-date while simultaneously carrying a safeguard against falling behind in the future (the *foreseeable* future at least, if there is such a thing). Seasoned consumers will surely get the message, which will prompt them to hurry up and remind them that there is no time to waste.

The message therefore implies a warning that will be left unheeded only at the greatest peril: however great your gain from promptly following the call, it won't last forever. Any insurance of security you acquire will need to be *renewed* once the 'coming months' are over. So watch this space. In the novel appropriately called *Slowness*, Milan Kundera reveals the intimate bond between speed and forgetting: 'the degree of speed is directly proportional to the intensity of forgetting.' Why so? Because if 'taking over the stage requires keeping other people off it', taking over that especially important stage known as 'public attention' (more exactly, the attention of that public earmarked to be recycled into consumers) requires keeping other objects of attention – other characters and other plots, including the plots mounted by the attention seekers yesterday – off it . . . 'Stages', Kundera reminds us, 'are floodlit only for the first few minutes.' In the liquid modern world, slowness portends social death. In the words of Vincent de Gaulejac, 'since all people progress, he who stays put will be inevitably separated from the others by a growing gap.'[3] The concept of 'exclusion' wrongly suggests someone's action – transporting its object away from the place it occupied; in fact, more often than not it is 'stagnation that excludes'.

Third, since not just one and only one, but 'half a dozen' looks are currently on offer, you are indeed free (even if – this word of caution is very much in order! – the range of the current offers draws an impassable limit round your choices). You can pick and choose your look. Choosing *as such* – choosing *some* look – is not at issue, since this is what you *must* do, and can desist and avoid doing only at peril of exclusion. Nor are you free to influence the set of options available to choose from: there are no other options left as all the realistic and advisable possibilities have been already preselected, pre-scripted and prescribed.

But never mind all these nuisances: the pressure of time, the necessity to ingratiate yourself in the eyes of the 'style pack' in case they turn theirs on you, notice and register your apparel and demeanour, or the strictly limited number of choices you can make (only 'half a dozen'). What really matters is that it is *you* who are now in charge. And be in charge you must: *choice* might be yours, but remember that *making a choice* is obligatory. Ellen Seiter points out that 'clothing, furniture, records, toys – all the things that we buy involve decisions and exercise of our own judgment and "taste"', but hastens to comment: 'Obviously we do not control what is available for us to choose from in the first place.'[4] All the same, in consumer culture choosing and freedom are two names of the same condition; and treating them as synonymous is correct at least in the sense that you can abstain from choosing only by at the same time surrendering your freedom.

The seminal departure that sets the *consumerist* cultural syndrome most sharply apart from its *productivist* predecessor, one that holds together the assembly of many different impulses, intuitions and proclivities and lifts the whole aggregate to the status of a coherent life programme, seems to be the *reversal of the values attached respectively to duration and transience*.

The consumerist cultural syndrome consists above all in the emphatic denial of the virtue of procrastination and of the propriety and desirability of the delay of satisfaction – those two axiological pillars of the society of producers ruled by the productivist syndrome.

In the inherited hierarchy of recognized values, the consumerist syndrome has degraded duration and elevated transience. It lifts the value of novelty above that of lastingness. It has sharply shortened the timespan separating not just the want from its fulfilment (as many observers, inspired or misled by credit agencies, have suggested), but also the birth moment of the want from the moment of its demise, as well as the realization of the usefulness and desirability of possessions from the perception of them as useless and in need of rejection. Among the objects of human desire, it has put the act of appropriation, to be quickly followed by waste disposal, in the place once accorded to the acquisition of possessions meant to be durable and to their lasting enjoyment.

Among human preoccupations, the consumerist syndrome puts precautions against the possibility of things (animate as much as inanimate) *outstaying their welcome* in place of the technique of *holding them fast* and of long-term (not to mention unending) attachment and commitment. It also radically shortens the life expectation of desire and the distance in time from desire to its gratification and from gratification to the waste disposal tip. *The 'consumerist syndrome' is all about speed, excess and waste.*

Fully fledged consumers are not finicky about consigning things to waste; *ils (et elles, bien sûr) ne regrettent rien.* As a rule, they accept the short lifespan of things and their preordained demise with equanimity, often with only thinly disguised relish, and sometimes with unalloyed joy and the celebration of victory. The most capable and quick-witted adepts of the consumerist art know that getting rid of things that have passed their use-by (read: enjoy-by) date is an event to be *rejoiced in.* To the masters of the consumerist art, the value of each and every object lies equally in its virtues and in its limitations. The shortcomings already known and those yet to be (inevitably) revealed thanks to their preordained and pre-designed obsolescence (or 'moral' as distinct from physical ageing, in Karl Marx's terminology) promise an imminent renewal and rejuvenation, new adventures, new sensations, new joys. In a society of consumers, perfection (if such a notion still holds any water) can be only a collective quality of the mass, of a multitude of objects of desire; the lingering urge to perfection now calls less for improvement in things than for their profusion and rapid circulation.

And so, let me repeat, a consumer society cannot but be a society of excess and profligacy – and so of redundancy and prodigal waste. The more fluid their life settings, the more objects of potential consumption are needed by the actors in order to hedge their bets and insure their actions against the pranks of fate (renamed in sociological parlance 'unanticipated consequences'). Excess, though, adds further to the uncertainty of choices which it was intended to abolish, or at least to mitigate or defuse – and so the excess already attained is unlikely ever to be excessive enough. Consumers' lives are bound to remain infinite successions of trials and errors. Theirs are lives of continuous experimentation – yet offering little hope of an *experimentum crucis* that might guide the experimenters on to a reliably mapped and signed land of certainty.

Hedge your bets; this is the golden rule of consumer rationality. In these life equations there are mostly variables and few if any constants, and the variables alter their values too often and too fast to keep track of their changes, let alone guess their future twists and turns.

The oft-repeated assurance 'this is a free country' means: it is up to you what sort of life you wish to live, how you decide to live it, and what kinds of choices you make in order to see your project through; blame yourself, and no one else, if all that does not result in the bliss you hoped for. It suggests the joy of emancipation is closely intertwined with the horror of defeat.

The two implications cannot be separated. Freedom is bound to bring untold risks of adventure flooding into the place vacated by the certainty of boredom. While it undoubtedly promises delightfully invigorating, since novel sensations, adventure is also a portent of the humiliation of failure and the loss of self-esteem caused by defeat. When the full scale of its risks, light-heartedly played down on the road to adventure, becomes evident once it is under way, boredom, the justly deprecated and berated bane of certainty, will tend to be forgotten and forgiven: its turn soon arrives for the scale and abomination of its discomforts to be played down.

The arrival of freedom, in the consumer choice avatar, tends to be viewed as an exhilarating act of *emancipation* – whether from harrowing obligations and irritating prohibitions, or from monotonous and stultifying routines. Soon after freedom has settled in and turned into another daily routine, a new kind of horror, no less frightening than the terrors the advent of freedom was to banish, makes memories of past sufferings and grudges pale: the horror of *responsibility*. The nights that follow days of obligatory routine are filled with dreams of freedom from constraint. The nights that follow days of obligatory choices are filled with dreams of freedom from responsibility.

It is therefore remarkable, but hardly surprising, that the two most powerful and persuasive cases for the necessity of 'society' (meaning in this case an authority endorsing and monitoring a comprehensive system of norms, rules, constraints, prohibitions and sanctions), advanced by philosophers from the start of the modern transformation, were prompted by recognition of the physical threats and spiritual burdens endemic to the condition of freedom.

The first case, articulated by Hobbes, elaborated at great length by Durkheim and, towards the middle of the twentieth century, turning into a tacit assumption incorporated into the common sense of social philosophy and science, presented societal coercion and the constraints imposed by normative regulation on individual freedom as a necessary, inevitable and in the end salutary and beneficial means of protecting human togetherness against 'war of all against all', and human individuals against life that is 'nasty, brutish and short'. The cessation of authoritatively administered social coercion, the advocates of this case argued (if such cessation were at all feasible, or even thinkable), would not liberate individuals; on the contrary, it would only make them unable to resist the morbid promptings of their own, essentially anti-social instincts. It would render them victims of a slavery much more horrifying than could possibly be produced by all the pressures of tough social realities. Freud would present socially exerted coercion and the resulting limitation of individual freedoms as the very essence of civilization: civilization without coercion would be unthinkable, given the 'pleasure principle' (such as the urge to seek sexual gratification or the inborn inclination of humans to laziness), which would guide individual conduct towards the wasteland of asociality if it were not constrained, trimmed and counterbalanced by the power-assisted and authority-operated 'reality principle'.

The second case for the necessity, indeed unavoidability, of socially operated normative regulation, and therefore also for social coercion constraining individual freedom, was founded on a quite opposite premise: that of the ethical challenge to which humans are exposed by the very presence of others, by the 'silent appeal of the face of the Other'. This challenge precedes all socially created and socially constructed, run and monitored ontological settings – which, if anything, try to neutralize, trim and limit the challenge of that otherwise boundless responsibility in order to make it endurable and liveable with. In this version, most fully elaborated by Emmanuel Levinas, but also by Knud Løgstrup in his concept of the 'unspoken [ethical] demand', society is seen primarily as a contraption for reducing the essentially unconditional and unlimited responsibility-for-the-other to a set of prescriptions and proscriptions more on a par with the human ability to cope. As Levinas suggests, the principal function of normative regulation, and also the paramount cause of its inevitability, is to make the essentially *unconditional* and *unlimited* responsibility for the Other both *conditional* (on selected, duly enumerated and clearly defined circumstances) and *limited* (to a selected group of 'others', considerably smaller than the totality of humanity, and most importantly narrower and so easier manageable than the indefinite sum total of 'others' who may eventually awaken in the subjects the sentiments of inalienable, and boundless, responsibility). In the vocabulary of Knud Løgstrup, a thinker remarkably close to Levinas's standpoint – insisting like Levinas on the primacy of ethics over the realities of life-in-society, and like him calling the world to account for failing to rise to the standards of ethical responsibility – one could say that society is an arrangement for rendering the otherwise stubbornly and vexingly silent (because unspecific) ethical demand audible (that is, specific and codified), thereby reducing the infinite multitude of options implied by such a command to a much narrower, manageable range of more or less clearly spelled out obligations.

The advent of consumerism has sapped the credibility and persuasive power of both cases – each in a different way, though for the same reason. The reason can be spotted in the ever more evident and still expanding process of dismantling the once comprehensive system of normative regulation. Ever larger chunks of human conduct have been released from explicitly social (not to mention endorsed by an authority and backed by official sanctions) patterning, supervision and policing, relegating an ever larger set of previously socialized responsibilities back to the responsibility of individual men and women. In a deregulated and privatized setting which is focused on consumer concerns and pursuits, the responsibility for choices, the actions that follow the choices and the consequences of such actions rests fully on the shoulders of individual actors. As Pierre Bourdieu signalled as long as two decades ago, coercion has by and large been replaced by stimulation, the once obligatory patterns of conduct by seduction, the policing of behaviour by PR and advertising, and normative regulation by the arousal of new needs and desires.

The advent of consumerism has apparently deprived the two cases previously discussed of a good deal of the credibility they were originally assumed to have, because the catastrophic consequences of abandoning or emaciating socially administered normative regulation, which they anticipated to be virtually inescapable, failed to materialize.

Though the profusion and intensity of antagonisms and open conflicts between individuals following the progressive deregulation and privatization of the functions tackled socially in the past, as well as the volume of damage they are capable of inflicting on the fabric of society, are all matters of an ongoing debate, the deregulated and privatized society of consumers is still far from, and apparently not coming much closer to, the terrifying vision of Hobbes. Neither did the explicit privatization of responsibility lead to the incapacitation of human subjects overwhelmed by the enormity of the challenge, as was implied by Levinas's or Løgstrup's visions – though the fate of ethical awareness and morally motivated behaviour does arouse numerous, serious and well-justified concerns.

It seems likely (though the jury is still out) that once they were exposed to the logic of commodity markets and left to their own choices, consumers found the power balance between the pleasure and the reality principles reversed. It is now the 'reality principle' that is assumed to be sitting on the defendant's bench. In case of a conflict between the two principles that were once deemed to stand in implacable opposition (by no means a foregone conclusion today, as I suggested earlier), it is the reality principle that would be most likely to be pressed and probably forced into retreat, self-limit and compromise. There seems little to be gained from the servicing of the hard and fast 'social facts' deemed indomitable and irresistible in Émile Durkheim's time – whereas catering for the infinitely expandable pleasure principle promises infinitely extendable gains and profits. The already blatant and still growing 'softness' and flexibility of liquid modern 'social facts' help to emancipate the search for pleasure from its past limitations (now censured as irrational) and open it fully to market exploitation.

The wars of recognition (alternatively interpretable as bids for legitimacy) waged in the aftermath of the pleasure principle's successive conquests tend to be brief and almost perfunctory, since their victorious outcome is in a great majority of cases a foregone conclusion. The main advantage of the 'reality principle' over the 'pleasure principle' used to rest on the large (social, supra-individual) resources commanded by the first when set against the much weaker (only individual) forces on which the second had to rely, but this has been greatly reduced, if not made null and void, as a result of the deregulation and privatization processes. It is now up to individual consumers to set (and fix, if that is feasible and wished for) the realities which could give flesh to the demands of the liquid version of the reality principle, as much as to pursue the targets dictated by the pleasure principle.

As to the case composed and advanced by Levinas: the task of reducing the supra-human boundlessness of ethical responsibility to the capacity of an ordinary human's sensitivity, power of judgement and ability to act also now tends to be, in all but a few selected areas, 'subsidiarized' to individual men and women. In the absence of an authoritative translation of the 'silent demand' into a finite inventory of obligations and proscriptions, it is now up to individuals to set the limits of their responsibility for other humans and to draw the line between what is plausible and what implausible among moral interventions – as well as to decide how far are they ready to go in sacrificing their own welfare for the sake of fulfilling their moral responsibilities to others.

Once transferred to individuals, that task becomes overwhelming, since the stratagem of hiding behind a recognized and apparently indomitable authority which will vouch to remove the responsibility (or at least a significant part of it) from their shoulders is no longer a viable or reliable option. Struggling with so daunting a task casts the actors into a state of permanent and incurable uncertainty; all too often, it leads to harrowing and demeaning self-reprobation. And yet the overall result of the privatization and subsidiarization of responsibility proves somewhat less incapacitating for the moral self and moral actors than Levinas and his disciples, myself included, would have expected. Somehow, a way has been found to mitigate their potentially devastating impact and limit the damage. There is, it appears, a profusion of commercial agencies eager to pick up the tasks abandoned by the 'great society' and to sell their services to bereaved, ignorant and confused consumers.

Under the deregulated and privatized regime, the formula of 'relief from responsibility' has remained much the same as it was in the earlier stages of modern history: the injection of a measure of genuine or putative clarity into a hopelessly opaque situation through the replacement (more exactly, concealment) of the mind-boggling complexity of the task with a finite and more or less comprehensive list of straightforward 'must do' and 'mustn't do' rules. Now as then, individual actors are nudged and cajoled to put their confidence in authorities trusted to find out what the silent demand demands them to do in this or that situation, and just how far (and no further) their unconditional responsibility obliges them to go under their present conditions.

The concepts of responsibility and responsible choice, which resided before in the semantic field of ethical duty and moral concern for the Other, have shifted or have been moved to the realm of self-fulfilment and the calculation of risks. In the process, 'the Other' as the trigger, the target and the yardstick of a responsibility recognized, assumed and fulfilled has all but disappeared from view, elbowed out or overshadowed by the actor's own self. 'Responsibility' now means, first and last, *responsibility to oneself* ('you owe this to yourself', 'you deserve it', as the traders in 'relief from responsibility' put it), while 'responsible choices' are, first and last, those moves serving the interests and satisfying the desires of the self.

The outcome is not much different from the 'adiaphorizing' effects of the stratagem practised by solid-modern bureaucracy, which was the substitution of 'responsibility *to*' (to the superior, to an authority, to the cause and its spokespeople) for the 'responsibility *for*' (for the Other's welfare and human dignity). Adiaphorizing effects (that is, proclaiming certain actions pregnant with moral choices 'ethically neutral' and exempting them from ethical evaluation and censure) tend, however, to be achieved these days mostly through replacing the 'responsibility *for others*' with 'responsibility *to oneself*' and 'responsibility *for oneself*' rolled into one. The collateral victim of the leap to the consumerist rendition of freedom is the Other as object of ethical responsibility and moral concern.

We can now return to the three messages signalled and briefly discussed at the beginning of this chapter.

All three messages announce, jointly and in unison, a state of emergency. Nothing new here, to be sure – only another reiteration of the oft-repeated reassurance that the perpetual vigilance, the constant readiness to go where go one must, the money that needs to be spent and the labours that have to be done on the way are all right and proper. Alerts (orange? red?) are switched on, new beginnings full of promise and new risks full of threats are signalled to lie ahead. All the paraphernalia required to make the right choices (to fulfil the inalienable responsibility *to* and *for* oneself), the suitable gadgets or routines and foolproof instructions on how to operate them to one's own best advantage are waiting somewhere close by, certainly within reach, and can be found with a modicum of wit and effort. The point is now, as before, never to miss that moment calling for action, lest the hapless, inattentive or absent-minded, neglectful or slothful actor drops behind instead of getting ahead of the 'style pack'. To neglect the listlessness of consumer markets and try to rely instead on instruments and routines that did the job well in the past simply won't do.

In her remarkable study of the fateful changes currently occurring in our perception and experience of time, Nicole Aubert points out the crucial role played by the 'state of emergency', and the mood or 'urgency' which that state, once declared, is expected and calculated to sow, disseminate and entrench.[5] She suggests that in present-day societies the state and the mood of 'emergency' meet a number of existential needs which in other known types of society tend to be either suppressed and left unprovided for, or are served through quite different stratagems. The new expedients which she traces back to the strategy of an intensely and extensively cultivated sentiment of *urgency* provide individuals and institutions alike with *illusionary*, though nevertheless quite effective, relief in their struggles to alleviate the potentially devastating consequences of the agonies of choice endemic in the condition of consumer freedom.

One of the most important illusions is provided by the momentary condensation of otherwise diffuse energy prompted by the alert. When it reaches the point of self-combustion, the accumulation of the power to act brings relief (albeit brief) from the pains of inadequacy haunting the daily life of consumers. The individuals Aubert spoke to and whom she observed at close quarters (individuals, let me explain, who happened to be trained and groomed in the arts of the consuming life, and who for that reason had grown intolerant of all and any frustration and could no longer cope with delay of the gratification they always expected to be immediate), 'having in a way ensconced themselves in the present moment, in a logic of "no delay", bathe in the illusion of potency to conquer time' by abolishing it (for a time!) altogether or at least by mitigating its frustrating impact.

It would be hard to exaggerate the healing or tranquillizing potency of such an illusion of mastery over time – the potency to dissolve the future in the present and encapsulate it in 'the now'. If, as Alain Ehrenberg convincingly argues,[6] most common human sufferings nowadays tend to grow from a surfeit of *possibilities*, rather than from a profusion of *prohibitions*, as they used to in the past, and if the opposition between the possible and the impossible has taken over from the antinomy of the allowed and the forbidden as the cognitive frame and essential criterion of the evaluation and choice of life strategy, it is only to be expected that depression arising from the terror of *inadequacy* will replace the neurosis caused by the horror of *guilt* (that is, of the charge of *nonconformity* that might follow a breach in the rules) as the most characteristic and widespread psychological affliction of the denizens of the society of consumers.

As the commonality of linguistic usages such as 'having time', 'lacking time', 'losing time' and 'gaining time' vividly demonstrates, concerns with matching the speed and the rhythm of the flow of time with an intensity of individual intentions and zeal of individual actions hold pride of place among our most frequent, energy-consuming and nerve-wracking preoccupations. Consequently, an inability to reach a perfect match between the effort and its reward (particularly a systematically revealed inability that saps belief in one's mastery over time) can be a prolific source of the 'inadequacy complex', that major affliction of liquid modern life. Indeed, among the common interpretations of failure, only a dearth of money can seriously compete nowadays with an absence of time.

There is hardly any other feat which can offer more effective (even if short-lived) relief to the complex of inadequacy than an extraordinarily intense effort undertaken in and under the influence of a state of emergency. As one of the high-ranking professionals interviewed by Aubert reported, at such moments he felt not quite a master of the world, but almost . . . He had the feeling of 'living stronger', and found enormous pleasure in that emotion. He derived pleasure, in his own words, from the sudden injection of adrenaline which gave him the impression of 'power over time, over complex processes, relations, interactions . . .' The healing capacity of the satisfaction experienced during a state of emergency could even outlive its cause. As another of Aubert's interviewees reported, the greatest benefit of tackling an urgent task was the sheer intensity of the lived moment. The content of the task and the cause of the urgency must have been purely incidental, inessential, since they were all but forgotten; what was remembered, however, and fondly, was the high level of intensity, and reassuring evidence, clinching proof even, of one's ability to rise to the challenge.

Another service which a life lived under recurrent or well-nigh perpetual states of emergency (even if they are artificially produced, or deceitfully proclaimed) can render to the sanity of our contemporaries is an updated version of Blaise Pascal's 'hare hunting', adjusted to a novel social setting. This is hunting that, in stark opposition to a hare already shot, cooked and consumed, leaves the hunter with little or no time to contemplate the brevity, emptiness, meaninglessness or vanity of their mundane pursuits, and by extension of their earthly life as a whole. Successive cycles of recuperating from the last alert and getting fit and gathering strength for the next, living once more through the moment of emergency and again recuperating from its tensions and the expenditure of energy that acting under pressure entailed, can fill all the potentially 'empty holes' of life which might otherwise be filled with the unbearable awareness of 'things ultimate', only provisionally repressed: things which, for the sake of sanity and the enjoyment of life, one would rather forget. To quote Aubert again:

Permanent busyness, with one urgency following another, gives the security of a full life or a 'successful career', sole proofs of

self-assertion in a world from which all references to the 'beyond'
are absent, and where existence, with its finitude, is the only certainty ... When they take action people think short-term – of
things to be done immediately or in the very near future ... All
too often, action is only an escape from the self, a remedy for the
anguish.[7]

And let me add that the more intense the action is, the more reliable its therapeutic potency. The deeper one sinks into the urgency
of an immediate task, the further away the anguish stays – or at
least it will feel less unbearable if the effort to keep it away fails.

Finally, there is one more crucial service which can be rendered
by lives dominated by alerts and urgencies and fully consumed by
efforts to cope with successive emergencies – this time to the
companies operating the consumerist economy, companies struggling for survival under conditions of cut-throat competition and
forced to adopt strategies likely to arouse tough resistance and
rebellion in their employees and ultimately to threaten the companies' ability to act effectively.

In the present day, the managerial practice of provoking an
atmosphere of urgency, or representing an arguably ordinary state
of affairs as a state of emergency, is more and more often recognized as a highly effective, and preferred, method of persuading
the managed to placidly accept even the most drastic changes
which strike at the heart of their ambitions and prospects – or,
indeed, at their very living. 'Declare a state of emergency – and
go on ruling' seems to be the ever more popular managerial recipe
for unchallenged domination and for getting away with the most
unpalatable and inflammatory assaults on the well-being of employees; or for getting rid of unwanted labour made redundant in
successive rounds of 'rationalization' or asset-stripping.

Neither learning nor forgetting can possibly escape the impact
of the 'tyranny of the moment' aided and abetted by the continuous state of emergency, and of time dissipated into a series of
disparate and apparently (though deceptively) unconnected 'new
beginnings'. Consuming life cannot be other than a life of rapid
learning, but it also needs to be a life of swift forgetting.

Forgetting is as important as learning, if not more important.
There is a 'must not' for every 'must', and which of the two reveals

the true objective of the breathtaking pace of renewal and removal, and which one is only an auxiliary measure to ensure that the objective is attained, is a hopelessly moot and chronically unresolved question. The sort of information/instruction likely to crop up most profusely in the 'fashion handbook' quoted earlier and in scores of similar ones is of the variety of the 'destination *this autumn* is 1960s Carnaby Street', or 'the current trend for Gothic is perfect *for this month*'. This autumn is of course something entirely different from the last summer, and this month is nothing like past months; and so what was perfect for last month is anything but perfect for this one, just as the destination of last summer lies light-years away from this autumn's destination. 'Ballet pumps'? 'Time to put them away.' 'Spaghetti straps'? 'They have no place this season.' 'Biros'? 'The world is a better place without them.' The call to 'open up your make-up bag and take a look inside' is likely to be followed by an exhortation that '*the coming season* is all about rich colours', followed closely by the warning that 'beige and its safe but dull relatives have had their day . . . Chuck it out, *right now*.' Obviously, 'dull beige' can't be pasted on the face simultaneously with 'deep rich colours'. One of the palettes must give way. Become redundant. Another waste, or 'collateral victim', of progress. Something to be disposed of. and fast.

The chicken or the egg question again . . . Must you 'chuck out' the beige in order to make your face ready to receive deep rich colours, or are the deep rich colours overflowing the supermarket cosmetics shelves in order to make sure that the supply of unused beige is indeed 'chucked out' 'right now'?

Many of the millions of women who are now chucking out the beige to fill their bags with deep rich colours would most probably say that sending the beige to the rubbish heap is a sad but unavoidable side-effect of make-up renewal and improvement, and a sad yet necessary sacrifice that has to be made to keep up with progress. But some shop managers of the thousands who order the restocking of department stores would probably admit in a moment of truth that filling the cosmetics shelves with rich deep colours was prompted by a need to shorten the useful life of the beiges – so keeping the traffic around the warehouses lively, the economy going, and profits rising. Is not GNP, the official index of the nation's well-being, measured by the amount of money changing hands? Is not economic growth propelled by the energy and activity of *consumers*? And the consumer who is not active in getting rid of used-up or obsolete possessions (indeed, of whatever is left of yesterday's purchases) is an oxymoron – like a wind that doesn't blow or river that doesn't flow . . .

It seems that *both* the above answers are right: they are complementary, not contradictory. In a society of consumers and in an era when 'life politics' is replacing the Politics that once boasted a capital 'P', the true 'economic cycle', the one that truly keeps the economy going, is the 'buy it, enjoy it, chuck it out' cycle. The fact that two such seemingly contradictory answers can be right at one and the same time is precisely the greatest feat of the society of consumers – and, arguably, the key to its astounding capacity for self-reproduction and expansion.

The life of a consumer, the consuming life, is not about acquiring and possessing. It is not even about getting rid of what was been acquired the day before yesterday and proudly paraded a day later. It is instead, first and foremost, about *being on the move*.

If Max Weber was right and the ethical principle of the producing life was (and always needed to be, if the aim was a producing life) the *delay* of gratification, then the ethical guideline of the consuming life (if the ethic of such a life can be presented in the form of a code of prescribed behaviour) has to be to avoid *staying satisfied*. For a kind of society which proclaims customer *satisfaction* to be its sole motive and paramount purpose, a *satisfied* consumer is neither motive nor purpose – but the most terrifying menace.

What applies to the society of consumers has to apply to its individual members as well. Satisfaction must be only a momentary experience, something to be feared rather than coveted if it lasts too long; lasting, once-and-for-all gratification has to seem to consumers anything but an attractive prospect; indeed, a catastrophe. As Dan Slater puts it, consumer culture 'associated satisfaction with economic stagnation: there must be no end to needs . . . (It) requires our needs both to be insatiable and yet always to look to commodities for their satisfaction.'[8] Or perhaps it could be put like this: we are pushed and/or pulled to look unstoppably for satisfaction, yet also to fear the kind of satisfaction that would stop us from looking . . .

As time goes by, we no longer in fact need pushing or pulling to feel like that and to act on those feelings. Nothing left to be desired? Nothing to chase after? Nothing to dream of with a hope of awakening to its truth? Is one bound to settle once and for all for what one *has* (and so also, by proxy, for what one *is*)? No longer anything new and extraordinary to push its way to the stage of attention, and nothing on that stage ever to be disposed and got rid of? Such a situation – hopefully short-lived – could only be called by one name: 'boredom'. The nightmares that haunt *Homo consumens* are things, inanimate or animate, or their shadows – the memories of things, animate or inanimate – that threaten to outstay their welcome and clutter up the stage . . .

It is not the creation of *new needs* (some call them 'artificial needs' albeit wrongly, since 'artificiality' is not a unique feature of 'new' needs: while they use natural human predispositions as their raw material, all needs in any society are given tangible, concrete form by the 'artifice' of social pressure) that constitutes the major preoccupation (and, as Talcott Parsons would say, the 'functional prerequisite') of the society of consumers. It is the playing down and derogation of *yesterday's needs* and the ridicule and uglification of their objects, now *passés*, and even more the discrediting of the very idea that consuming life ought to be guided by the *satisfaction of needs* that keep the consumer economy and consumerism alive. Beige make-up, last season a sign of boldness, is now not just a colour going out of fashion, but a dull and ugly colour, and moreover a shameful stigma and brand of ignorance, indolence, ineptitude, or all-round inferiority, with the act which not that long ago used to signal rebellion, daring and 'staying ahead of the style-pack' rapidly turning into a symptom of sloth or cowardice ('This is not make-up, it's a security blanket'), a sign of falling behind the pack, perhaps even becoming down and out . . .

Let us recall that according to the verdict of consumerist culture those individuals who settle for a finite assembly of needs, go solely by what they believe they need, and never look for new needs that might arouse a pleasurable yearning for satisfaction are *flawed consumers* – that is, the variety of social outcast specific to the society of consumers. The threat and fear of ostracism and exclusion also hovers over those who are satisfied with the identity they possess and will settle for what their 'significant others' take them to be.

The consumerist culture is marked by a constant pressure to be *someone else*. Consumer markets focus on the prompt devaluation of their past offers, to clear a site in public demand for new ones to fill. They breed dissatisfaction with the products used by consumers to satisfy their needs – and they also cultivate constant disaffection with the acquired identity and the set of needs by which such an identity is defined. Changing identity, discarding the past and seeking new beginnings, struggling to be born again – these are promoted by that culture as a *duty* disguised as a privilege.

What, given the infinity of consumerist vistas, makes the 'pointillization' or 'punctuation' of time (see chapter 1) a most attractive novelty and a way of being-in-the-world of a kind that will surely be gladly learned and practised with zeal is the double promise: of pre-empting the future, and of disempowering the past.

Such a double act is, after all, the ideal of liberty (I was about to write the '*modern* ideal of liberty', but realized that the added qualifier would make the expression pleonastic: what was called 'liberty' in premodern settings would not pass the test of freedom by modern standards and so would not be considered 'liberty' at all).

When combined, the promise of emancipating actors from the constraints on choice imposed by the past (the kinds of constraints particularly strongly resented for their nasty habit of growing in volume and stiffening up as the 'past' fills relentlessly with ever thicker sediments of ever longer stretches of life history), and the permission to put paid to worries about the future (and more exactly about the future consequences of current actions, with their hotly resented power to dash current hopes, revoke or reverse the value of present verdicts and retrospectively devalue currently celebrated successes) augur a complete, unrestrained, well-nigh 'absolute' freedom. The society of consumers offers such freedom to a degree unheard of and indeed downright inconceivable in any other society on record.

Let us consider first the uncanny feat of disabling the past. It boils down to just one, but a truly miraculous change in the human condition: the newly invented (though advertised as newly discovered) facility of being 'born again'. Thanks to this invention, it is not only cats that have nine lives. Into one abominably short visit on earth, a visit not that long ago bewailed for its loathsome brevity and not radically lengthened since, humans-turned-consumers are now offered the chance to cram many lives: an endless series of new beginnings. A whole series of families, careers, identities. It now takes just a small scratch to start from scratch . . . Or at least it seems that it does.

One of the manifestations of the present attraction of 'serial births' – of life as an unending string of 'new beginnings' – is the widely noted and astounding expansion of cosmetic surgery. Not so long ago it was vegetating on the margin of the medical profession as a repair shop of last resort for the few men and women who had been cruelly disfigured by a freak combination of genes, by burns that wouldn't heal, or ugly scars that wouldn't fade; now, for the millions who can afford the cost, it has turned into a routine instrument of the perpetual remaking of the visible self. *Perpetual* indeed: the creation of a 'new and improved' look is no longer viewed as a one-off affair; the changing meaning of 'improvement' and so the need (and, of course, the availability) of further rounds of surgery to efface the traces of the previous ones are built into the idea as one of its paramount attractions (as reported in the *Guardian* of 16 May 2006, 'Transform', 'the leading British plastic surgery company with eleven centres around the country', offers its clients 'loyalty cards' to be used for repeat surgery). Plastic surgery is not about the removal of a blemish, or reaching an ideal shape denied by nature or fate, but about keeping up with fast-changing standards, retaining one's market value and discarding an image that has outlived its utility or charm so that a new public image can be put in its place – in a package deal with (hopefully) a new identity and (this for sure) a new beginning. In his brief but thorough survey of the spectacular rise of the cosmetic surgery business, Anthony Elliott observes:

Today's surgical culture promotes a fantasy of the body's infinite plasticity. The message from the makeover industry is that there's nothing to stop you reinventing yourself however you choose, but for the same reason, your surgically enhanced body is unlikely to make you happy for long. For today's reshapings of the body are only fashioned with the short-term in mind – until 'the next procedure' . . . Cheaper and more widely available than ever before, cosmetic surgery is fast becoming a lifestyle choice.

Each new beginning may take you only so far, and no further; each new beginning augurs many new beginnings to come. Each moment has a vexing tendency to turn into the past – and in no time its own turn to be disabled will arrive. The ability to disable the past is after all the deepest meaning of the promise of enablement carried by the goods offered by consumer markets.

The world inhabited by consumers is perceived by its inhabitants as a huge container of spare parts. The warehouse of spare parts is constantly and lavishly stocked, and trusted to be forever replenished if it temporarily runs short of supplies. No longer is one supposed to settle for what one has or what one is, and make do with both, reconciling oneself to the absence of other options and trying, for lack of alternatives, to make the best use of what the fate has offered. If some part (of the set of implements in daily use, of the current network of human contacts, of one's own body or its public presentation, of one's self/identity and its publicly presented image) loses its public allure or market value, it needs to be excised, pulled out and replaced by a 'new and improved', or just fresher and not yet worn out 'spare part'; if not DIY or home-made, then (and preferably) factory-made and shop-supplied.

It is for such a perception of the world, and their *modus operandi* in it, that the consumers of consumer society are trained from birth and throughout their lives. The expedient of selling the next item at a lower price on condition that the similar item bought previously is returned to the shop 'after use' is ever more widely practised by companies trading in household goods; but Lesław Hostyński, an insightful analyst of the values of consumer culture, has listed and described a long series of other stratagems deployed in the marketing of consumer goods in order to discourage the young (and ever younger) adepts of consumerism from developing a long-term attachment to anything they buy and enjoy.[9] Mattel, for instance, the company that flooded the toy market with Barbie dolls, reaching 1.7 billion dollars worth of sales in 1996 alone, promised young consumers they would sell them the next Barbie at a discount if they brought their currently used specimen back to the shop once it was 'used *up*'. The 'disposal mentality', that indispensable complement of the 'spare-part vision' of the (commoditized) world, was first signalled by Alvin Toffler in his *Shock of the Future* as a kind of spontaneous, grass-roots development, but has since become a major objective of companies in educating their prospective clients from early child-hood and throughout their consuming life.

Exchanging one Barbie doll for a 'new and improved' one leads to a life of liaisons and partnerships shaped and lived after a pattern of rent-purchase. As Pascal Lardellier suggests, the 'senti-mental logic' tends to become ever more saliently consumerist:[10] it is aimed at the reduction of all sorts of risks, the categorization of the items searched for, an effort to define precisely the features of the sought-after partner that can be deemed adequate to the aspirations of the searcher. The underlying conviction is that it is possible to compose the object of love from a number of clearly specified and measurable physical and social qualities and character traits. According to the precepts of such 'marketing *amoureux*' (the term coined by Lardellier), if the love object sought fails on one or several scores, the prospective 'buyer' of the 'love object' should desist from the 'purchase', as he or she would certainly do in the case of all other goods on offer; if, however, a failure is revealed *after* the 'purchase', the failed object of love, like all other market goods, needs to be discarded and duly replaced. Jonathan Keene saw the conduct of clients cruising over the internet in search of the composite ideal of a partner as giving the impression of an 'emotionally removed activity', 'as if people were chops in a butcher's window.'[11]

Being 'born again' means that the previous birth(s), together with their consequences, has (have) been, for all practical intents and purposes, annulled.

Each successive 'new beginning' (another incarnation) feels reassuringly, even if deceitfully, like the arrival of a – always wist-fully dreamt of, though never before deemed to be experienced (let alone practised) – potency of the kind proclaimed by Shestov to be God's exclusive prerogative and defining trait: Leon Shestov, the eminent Russian-French existentialist philosopher, argued that the power to annul the past (to make it, for instance, so that Socrates had never been forced to drink hemlock) was the ultimate sign of God's omnipotence. The potency of reshaping past events or rendering them null and void can override and disarm the power of causal determination, and so the power of the past to cut down the options of the present can be radically curtailed, perhaps even abolished altogether. What one was yesterday will no longer bar the possibility of becoming someone totally different today – nor prevent the prospect of another avatar in the future that will efface the present – its past.

Since each point in time, let's recall, is supposed to be full of unexplored potential, and each potential is supposed to be original and unique, never to be copied at any other time-point, the number of ways in which one can alter (or at least try to alter) oneself is genuinely uncountable: indeed, it even dwarfs the astonishing multitude of permutations and mind-boggling variety of forms and likenesses which the haphazard meetings of genes have managed thus far, and are likely to manage in the future, to produce in the human species. Andrzej Stasiuk, the perceptive observer of the way we live nowadays, has suggested that the multitude, nay infinity of options comes close to the awe-inspiring capacity of eternity, in which, as we know, *everything* may sooner or later happen and *everything* can sooner or later be done; now, however, that wondrous potency of eternity has been packed into the not at all eternal span of a single human life.

Consequently, the feat of disarming the power of the past to reduce subsequent choices, together with the facility of 'another birth' thereby created (that is, another incarnation), rob eternity of its most seductive attraction. In the pointillized time of the society of consumers, *eternity is no longer a value and an object of desire*. The one quality which more than any other accorded it its unique and truly monumental value and made it an object of dreams has been excised, compressed and condensed into a 'big bang'-style experience and *grafted on to the moment* – any moment. Accordingly, the liquid modern 'tyranny of the moment', with its precept of *carpe diem*, replaces the premodern tyranny of eternity with its motto of *memento mori*.

In his book with the title that tells it all, Thomas Hylland Eriksen picks the 'tyranny of the moment' as the most conspicuous feature of contemporary society, and arguably its most seminal novelty:

> The consequences of extreme hurriedness are overwhelming: both the past and the future as mental categories are threatened by the

tyranny of the moment . . . (E)ven the 'here and now' is threatened since the next moment comes so quickly that it becomes difficult to live in the present.[12]

A paradox indeed, and an inexhaustible source of tension: the more voluminous and capacious the moment becomes, the smaller (briefer) it is; as its potential contents swell, its dimensions shrink. 'There are strong indications that we are about to create a kind of society where it becomes nearly impossible to think a thought that is more than a couple of inches long.'[13] But contrary to the popular hopes promoted by the promises of the consumer market, changing one's identity, were it at all plausible, would require much more than a thought a couple of inches long.

When it undergoes the 'pointillization' treatment, the experience of time is cut off on both sides. Its interfaces with both the past *and* the future turn into gaps – with no bridges, and hopefully unbridgeable. Ironically, in the age of instant and effortless connection and the promise of being constantly 'in touch', there is a desire to suspend communication between the experience of the moment and whatever may precede or follow it, or better yet irreparably break it off. The gap behind should see to it that the past is never allowed to catch up with the running self. The gap ahead is a condition of living the moment to the full, of abandoning oneself totally and unreservedly to its (admittedly fleeting) charm and seductive power: an act that would be hardly, if at all, feasible were the moment currently being lived through contaminated with worry about mortgaging the future.

Ideally, each moment will be shaped after the pattern of credit card use, a radically depersonalized act: in the absence of face-to-face intercourse it is easier to forget the unpleasantness of any repayment the moment of pleasure may incur, or rather never think about it in the first place. No wonder the banks, eager to get cash moving and to earn still more money than they would if the cash available for spending was allowed to lay idle, prefer their clients to finger credit cards instead of buttonholing branch managers.

Following Bertman's terminology, Elżbieta Tarkowska, a prominent chronosociologist in her own right, has developed the concept of 'synchronic humans', who 'live solely in the present' and who 'pay no attention to past experience or future consequences of their actions', a strategy which 'translates into the absence of bonds with the others'. The 'presentist culture' 'puts a premium on speed and effectiveness, while favouring neither patience nor perseverance.'[14]

We may add that it is this frailty and apparently easy disposability of individual identities and interhuman bonds that are represented in contemporary culture as the substance of individual freedom. One choice that such freedom would neither recognize, nor grant, nor allow is the resolve (or indeed the ability) to persevere in holding to the identity already constructed, that is in the kind of activity which also presumes, and necessarily entails, the preservation and security of the social network on which that identity rests while it actively reproduces it.

In *Liquid Love* I attempted to analyse the growing frailty of interhuman bonds. I concluded that human bonds nowadays tend to be viewed – with a mixture of rejoicing and anxiety – as frail, easily falling apart and as easy to be broken as they are to tie.

If they are viewed with rejoicing, it is because such frailty mitigates the risks assumed to be present in every interaction, the danger of a present knot being tied too firmly for future comfort, and the probability of allowing it to ossify into one of those things that are 'past their time', once attractive but now repulsive, cluttering up the habitat and cramping the freedom to explore the endless cavalcade of moments pregnant with new and improved attractions.

And if they are viewed with anxiety, it is because the brittleness, temporariness and revocability of mutual commitments are themselves a source of awesome risks. The predispositions and intentions of other human beings present and active inside the lifeworld of each individual are, after all, unknown variables. They can't be taken for granted, counted on or safely predicted – and the resulting uncertainty puts a huge and ineffaceable question mark on the pleasures derived from any current bond well before the anticipated satisfactions have tasted in full and truly exhausted. The rising fragility of human bonds is therefore experienced all along, from the moment of their conception and long after their demise, as a blessing mixed with a curse. It does not reduce the sum total of apprehension, only distributes the anxieties in a different way, and their future meanders are virtually impossible to foresee, let alone to prescribe and control.

Some observers of the contemporary scene, notably Manuel Castells and Scott Lash, welcome the new technology of virtual bonding and unbonding as promising alternative and in some ways superior forms of sociality; as a possibly effective cure, or preventive medicine, against the menace of consumer-style loneliness; and as a boost for consumer-style freedom (that is, the freedom to make and unmake one's choices) – an alternative form of sociality which goes some way towards reconciling the conflicting demands of liberty and security. Castells writes of 'networking individualism', Scott Lash of 'communicational bonds'. Both however seem to take *pars pro toto,* even if each focuses on a different part of the complex, ambivalent totality.

If looked on from the standpoint of the missed part, the 'network' feels worryingly like a wind-blown dune of quicksand rather than a building site for reliable social bonds. When electronic communication networks enter the habitat of the individual consumer they are equipped from the start with a safety device: the possibility of instant, trouble-free and (hopefully) painless disconnection – of cutting off communication in a way that would leave parts of the network unattended and deprive them of relevance, together with their power to be a nuisance. It is that safety device, and not the facility of getting in touch, let alone of staying together permanently, that endears the electronic substitute for face-to-face socializing to men and women trained to operate in a market-mediated world. In such a world, it is the act of getting rid of the unwanted, much more than the act of getting hold of the desired, that is the meaning of individual freedom. The safety device that allows instantaneous disconnection on demand perfectly fits the essential precepts of the consumerist culture; but social bonds, and the skills needed to tie them and service them, are its first and principal collateral casualties.

Considering that 'virtual space' is fast turning into the natural habitat of current and aspiring members of the knowledge classes, it is little wonder that quite a few academics also tend to greet the internet and the world wide web as a promising and welcome alternative or replacement for the wilting and fading orthodox institutions of political democracy, known these days to command ever less interest and still less commitment on the part of citizens.

For present and aspiring members of the knowledge classes, to quote Thomas Frank, 'politics becomes primarily an exercise in individual auto-therapy, an individual accomplishment, not an effort aimed at the construction of a movement'[15] – a means to inform the world of their own virtues, as documented for instance by iconoclastic messages stuck to car windows or by ostentatious displays of conspicuously 'ethical' consumption. Theorizing the internet as a new and improved form of politics, surfing the world wide web as a new and more effective form of political engagement, and accelerated connection to the internet and the rising speed of surfing as advances in democracy look suspiciously like so many glosses on the ever more common and ever more depoliticized life practices of the knowledge class, and above all on their keen concern with an honourable discharge from the 'politics of the real'.

Against such a background of choral praise, Jodi Dean's blunt verdict is all the more resounding: that present-day communication technologies are 'profoundly depoliticizing', that 'communication functions fetishistically today: as a disavowal of a more fundamental political disempowerment or castration', that

> the technological fetish is 'political' . . . enabling us to go about the rest of our lives relieved of the guilt that we might not be doing our part and secure in the belief that we are after all informed, engaged citizens . . . We don't have to assume political responsibility because . . . the technology is doing it for us . . . (It) lets us think that all we need is to universalize a particular technology and then we will have a democratic or reconciled social order.[16]

Reality stands, as it were, in stark opposition to the sanguine and cheerful portrait of it painted by 'communication fetishists'. The powerful flow of information is not a confluent of the river of democracy, but an insatiable intake intercepting its contents and channelling them away into magnificently huge, yet stale and stagnant artificial lakes. The more powerful that flow is, the greater the threat of the riverbed drying up. The world servers store information so that the new liquid modern culture can substitute forgetting for learning as the major driving force of consumers' life pursuits. Servers suck in and store the imprints of dissent and protest so that liquid modern politics can roll on unaf-

fected and unabated – substituting soundbites and photo opportunities for confrontation and argument.

The currents flowing away from the river are not easily reversed
and returned to the riverbed: Bush and Blair could go to war
under false pretences with no *dearth* of websites calling their
bluff. Appropriately, news presenters prefer (or are preferred) to
tell all there is to be told about the state of politics while standing
up, as if caught in the midst of some altogether different business
or having stopped for a moment on their way elsewhere. Sitting
down at a desk would suggest that the news has a more durable
significance than it is intended to carry, and more profound reflection than the consumers at the other end of the channel of mass
communication, each engaged in her or his own business, are
supposed to be able to bear.

As far as 'real politics' is concerned, as dissent travels towards
electronic warehouses it is sterilized, defused and made irrelevant.
Those who stir the waters in the storage lakes may congratulate
themselves on their verve and sprightliness, testifying to their
fitness, but those in the corridors of real power will hardly be
forced to pay attention. They will only be grateful to the state-of-
the-art communication technology for the job it performs in
siphoning off potential troubles and taking apart the barricades
erected across their path before the builders of those barricades
have had time to put them together, let alone to summon the
people needed to defend them.

Real politics and virtual politics run in opposite directions, and
the distance between them grows as the self-sufficiency of each
benefits from the absence of the other's company. Jean Baudrillard's age of simulacra did not cancel the difference between
genuine stuff and its reflection, between real and virtual realities;
it only dug a precipice between them – easy for the internauts to
leap over, but increasingly difficult for the present, and even more
for the aspiring, citizens to bridge.

As Christopher Lasch bitterly commented just before PCs and
mobile telephones started to colonize consumers' private and intimate worlds, people who 'live in cities and suburbs where shopping malls have replaced neighbourhoods . . . are not likely to
reinvent communities just because the state has proved such an
unsatisfactory substitute.'[17] That verdicts still holds, well after the

colonization spread to the furthest nooks and crannies of the planet with the speed of a forest fire.

In his recent study of contemporary obsessions focused on identity (and particularly of the attention attached nowadays to composing and dismantling identities), Kwame Anthony Appiah tries to grasp the curious dialectics of 'the collective' and 'the individual', or of 'belonging' and 'self-assertion'; dialectics that makes efforts at self-identification ultimately ineffective yet (perhaps for that very reason) unstoppable and unlikely ever to run short of vigour.[18] He suggests that if, for instance, the fact of being an Afro-American affects the shape of the self which someone is struggling to express and put on public display, he or she enters that struggle in the first place and seeks recognition for his or her Afro-Americanism because of feeling the need to have a self suitable for being shown and publicly displayed. Circumstantial and contingent ascriptive determinations may explain the selection made between selves suitable for display, but hardly the very attention one attaches to making *a* selection and then making it publicly visible; even less does it explain the zeal with which the effort to make it visible is undertaken.

Even if the self he or she is struggling to display and get recognized is deemed by the actor to precede, pre-empt and predetermine the choice of individual identity (ethnic, race, religious and gender ascriptions claim to belong to that category of self), *it is the urge of selection and the effort to make the choice publicly recognizable that constitutes the self-definition of the liquid modern individual*. That effort would have hardly been undertaken if the identity in question was indeed endowed with the determining power it claims and/or is believed to possess.

In the liquid modern society of consumers no identities are gifts at birth, none is 'given', let alone given once and for all and in a secure fashion. Identities are projects: tasks yet to be undertaken, diligently performed and seen through to infinitely remote completion. Even in the case of those identities that pretend and/or are supposed to be 'given' and non-negotiable, the obligation to undertake an individual effort to appropriate them and then struggle daily to hold on to them is presented and perceived as the principal requirement and indispensable condition of their 'givenness'. The neglectful, lukewarm or slothful, let alone the infidel, the two-minded and treacherous, will be denied the right to invoke their birthright.

Rather than a gift (let alone a 'free gift', to recall the pleonastic phrase coined by marketing advisers), identity is a sentence to lifelong hard labour. For the producers of avid and indefatigable consumers and for the sellers of consumer goods it is also an inexhaustible source of capital – a source that tends to grow bigger with each scoop. Once set in motion in early childhood, the composing and dismantling of identity becomes a self-propelling and self-invigorating activity.

Remember that consumers are driven by the need to 'commoditize' themselves – remake themselves into attractive commodities – and pressed to deploy all the usual stratagems and expedients of marketing practice for that purpose. Obliged to find a market niche for the valuables they may possess or hope to develop, they must acutely watch the vacillations of what is demanded and what offered, and follow the market trends: an unenviable, often utterly exhausting task, given the notorious volatility of consumer markets. Markets do all they can to render that task ever more daunting, while simultaneously doing all they can to supply (at a price) shortcuts, DIY kits and patented formulae to relieve customers of the burden, or at least to convince them that the coveted relief has indeed arrived – for a moment, at any rate.

Two expedients in particular play a major role in relieving the pains of identity building and identity dismantling in the society of consumers.

The first is what I have called elsewhere 'cloakroom communities' (like the gathering of theatre viewers in a cloakroom as they all leave their coats or anoraks for the duration of the performance they have come to watch, singly or in small groups, from their respective seats). These are ghost communities, phantom communities, ad hoc communities, carnival communities – the kinds of communities one feels one joins simply by being where others are present, or by sporting badges or other tokens of shared intentions, style or taste; and *fixed-term* (or at least acknowledged as temporary) communities from which one 'falls out' once the crowd disperses, while being free to leave before that at any time should one's interest begin to wane.

Cloakroom communities do not call for entry or exit permissions, or have offices that could issue them, and even less are they entitled to define the binding criteria of eligibility for applying. The modality of 'community membership' is fully subjective; it is the 'momentary *experience* of community' that counts. In a consumer existence smarting under the tyranny of the moment and measured by pointillist time the facility to join in and to leave at will gives that experience of the phantom, ad hoc community a clear advantage over the uncomfortably solid, constraining and demanding 'real thing'.

The tickets to performances, the badges and other publicly displayed tokens of identity are all market supplied; this is the second of the two expedients provided by the modality of consumerist life to relieve the burden of identity construction and deconstruction. Consumer goods are seldom if ever identity-neutral; they tend to come complete with 'identity supplied' (just like toys and electronic gadgets sold with 'batteries supplied'). The work dedicated to the construction of identities fit for public display and publicly recognizable, as well as obtaining the coveted 'experience of community', requires primarily shopping skills.

With a mind-boggling profusion of brand new, eye-catching and alluring identities never further from reach than the nearest shopping mall, the chances of any particular identity being placidly accepted as the ultimate one, calling for no further overhaul or replacement, are equal to the proverbial survival chances of a snowball in hell. Indeed, why settle for what one has already finished building, warts and all, if new self-assembly kits promise excitements never before experienced and – who knows? – throw open gates leading to delights never before enjoyed? 'If not fully satisfied, return goods to the shop': is it not the first principle of the consuming life strategy?

Joseph Brodsky, the Russian-American philosopher-poet, vividly described the kind of life set in motion and prompted by the obsessive and compulsive shop-mediated search for a continually updated, re-formed identity, with new births and new beginnings:

> you'll be bored with your work, your spouses, your lovers, the view from your window, the furniture or wallpaper in your room, your thoughts, yourselves. Accordingly, you'll try to devise ways of escape. Apart from the self-gratifying gadgets mentioned before, you may take up changing jobs, residence, company, country,

climate, you may take up promiscuity, alcohol, travel, cooking lessons, drugs, psychoanalysis . . . In fact, you may lump all these together, and for a while that may work. Until the day, of course, when you wake up in your bedroom amid a new family and a different wallpaper, in a different state and climate, with a heap of bills from your travel agent and your shrink, yet with the same stale feeling toward the light of day pouring through your window . . .[19]

Andrzej Stasiuk, an outstanding Polish novelist and particularly perceptive analyst of the contemporary human condition, suggests that 'the possibility of becoming someone else' is a present-day substitute for the now largely discarded and uncared-for salvation or redemption. One would add: a substitute far superior to the original, since it is instantaneous rather than being vexingly slow in coming, and multiple as well as revocable instead of being the 'one and only' and ultimate.

> Applying various techniques, we can change our bodies and re-shape them according to a different pattern . . . When browsing through glossy magazines, one gets the impression that they mostly tell one story – about the ways in which one can remake one's personality, starting from diets, surroundings, homes, and up to a rebuilding of its psychological structure, often code-named the proposition to 'be yourself.'[20]

Sławomir Mrożek, a Polish writer of a worldwide fame with first-hand experience of many lands, agrees with Stasiuk's hypothesis. Mrożek compares the world we inhabit to

> a market-stall filled with fancy dresses and surrounded by crowds seeking their 'selves' . . . One can change dresses without end, so what a wondrous liberty the seekers enjoy. . . . Let's go on searching for our real selves, it's smashing fun – on condition that the real self will be never found. Because if it were, the fun would end . . .[21]

The dream of making uncertainty less daunting and happiness more profound, while calling for less sacrifice and no exhausting effort day in day out, simply by using the facility of ego-change, and of changing one's ego by donning dresses that don't stick to the skin and so are unlikely to pre-empt further change, lies at the heart of the consumers' obsession with the manipulation of identities. In the case of self-definition and self-construction, as in all other life pursuits, the consumerist culture remains true to its character and forbids a final settlement and any consummate, perfect gratification that calls for no further improvement. In the activity called 'identity building', the true, even if secret, purpose is the discarding and disposal of failed or not fully successful products. And it is by the promised facility of discarding and replacement that products are measured as failed or not fully successful. No wonder that, as Siegfried Kracauer presciently suggested, in our era the 'integrated personality undoubtedly belongs among the favourite superstitions of modern psychology.'[22]

Reshuffling identities, discarding the ones previously constructed and experimenting with new ones directly result from life spent in pointillist time, when every moment is pregnant with unexplored opportunities which are likely to die unrecognized and intestate if they are untried. They are, however, steadily turning into activities desired and conducted for their own sake. Since no amount of experiments are likely to exhaust the infinity of chances, the vigour of exploration and impatience with the disappointing results of past trials will probably never diminish. The natural limits imposed on the duration and range of experimentation – by the finitude of an individual life, by the scarcity of the resources required for the production of new identities, by the limited sizes of the habitats where identities are put to repetitive tests of public recognition, or by the resistance or incredulity of the significant others whose approval is crucial for recognition to be granted – tend to be resented and viewed as illegitimate and thus unacceptable constraints imposed on the individual liberty to choose.

Fortunately for the addicts of identity alteration, of new beginnings and multiple births, the internet opens opportunities denied or closed off in 'real life'. The wondrous advantage of the virtual life space over the 'offline' one(s) consists in the possibility to get the identity recognized without actually practising it.

The internauts seek, find and enjoy the shortcuts leading directly from the play of fantasy to the social (albeit also only virtual) acceptance of the make-believe. As Francis Jauréguiberry suggests, transferring the experiments in self-identification into virtual space feels like an emancipation from the vexing constraints filling the offline realm: 'Internauts may experiment, again and again from scratch, with new *selves* of their choice – with no fear of sanctions.'[23] No wonder that more often than not the identities assumed during a visit to the internet world of instant connections and disconnections on demand are of a kind that would be physically or socially untenable offline. They are, fully and truly, 'carnival identities', but thanks to the laptop or mobile telephone the carnivals, and particularly the privatized ones among them, can be enjoyed at any time – and most importantly at a time of one's own choosing.

In the carnivalesque game of identities, offline socializing is revealed for what it in fact is in the world of consumers: a rather cumbersome and not particularly enjoyable burden, tolerated and suffered because unavoidable, since recognition of the chosen identity needs to be achieved in long and possibly interminable effort – with all the risks of bluffs being called or imputed which face-to-face encounters necessarily entail. Cutting off that burdensome aspect of the recognition battles is, arguably, the most attractive asset of the internet masquerade and confidence game. The 'community' of internauts seeking substitute recognition does not require the chore of socializing and is thereby relatively free from risk, that notorious and widely feared bane of the offline battles for recognition.

Another revelation is the redundancy of the 'other' in any role other than as a token of endorsement and approval. In the internet game of identities, the 'other' (the addressee and sender of messages) is reduced to his or her hard core of a thoroughly manipulable instrument of self-confirmation, stripped of most or all of the unnecessary bits irrelevant to the task still (however grudgingly and reluctantly) tolerated in offline interaction. To quote Jauréguiberry once more:

> In the search for successful self-identification, the self-manipulating individuals maintain a very instrumental relationship with their conversationalists. The latter are admitted solely for the sake of certifying the manipulators' existence – or more exactly for the sake of allowing the manipulators to topple over their 'virtual selves' into reality. The others are sought for no other purpose than for attesting, comforting and flattering the internauts' virtual selves.

In the internet-mediated identification game, the Other is, so to speak, disarmed and detoxified. The Other is reduced by the internaut to what really counts: to the status of the instrument of one's own self-endorsement. The unprepossessing necessity to grant the Other's autonomy and originality, and to approve the Other's claims to an identity of their own, not to mention the off-putting need for durable bonds and commitments, unavoidable in the offline battles for recognition, are all eliminated or at least kept off-limits for the duration. Virtual socializing proceeds after the pattern of marketing, and the electronic tools of that kind of socializing are made to the measure of marketing techniques.

Its great attraction is the unalloyed pleasure of make-believe, with the unsavoury bit of the 'make' all but excised from the list of the maker's worries since it remains invisible to the 'believers'.

4

Collateral Casualties of Consumerism

The newly coined and instantly popular concepts of 'collateral damage', 'collateral casualties' and 'collateral victims' belong to the barrister's vocabulary and are rooted in the pragmatics of legal defence, even if they were first deployed by military spokesmen in their press briefings and transferred to journalist language and then to the vernacular from there.

Though with a wink at the widely described phenomenon of the 'unanticipated consequences' of human actions, 'collaterality' subtly shifts the emphasis. The shared meaning of all three of the concepts listed above is to excuse harm-causing actions, to justify them and exempt them from punishment, on the strength of their unintentionality. As Stanley Cohen might say, they belong to the linguistic arsenal of 'states of denial': denial of *responsibility* – *moral* responsibility as well as *legal*. For instance (and such instances have been increasingly common of late), a dozen or so women and children had their lives violently interrupted, or were maimed for life, by a smart missile meant to hit a single man suspected of training others or being trained himself in the role of suicide bomber; in the next press briefing by a military spokesman, the death of women and children will be mentioned, well after the hitting of the appointed targets has been described in detail, as 'collateral damage' – as a kind of harm for which no one could be brought to trial, since the local residents and passersby who were killed or wounded did not figure among the targets aimed at by those who launched the missile and those who ordered it to be launched.

The moot question, of course, is whether 'unanticipated' means necessarily 'impossible to anticipate', and yet more to the point, whether 'unintentional' stands for 'impossible to calculate' and so 'impossible to intentionally avoid', or for a mere indifference and callousness in those who did the calculations and did not care enough about the avoiding. Once such a question is explicitly asked, it becomes clear that whatever answer the investigation of a particular case may suggest, there are good reasons to suspect that what the invoking of the 'unintentionality' argument intends to deny or exonerate is *ethical blindness*, conditioned or deliberate. Purely and simply, killing a few alien women and children was not considered an excessive price to pay for blowing up or even trying to blow up one would-be terrorist. When elephants fight, pity the grass; but the elephants will be the last to pity the grass. Were they able to speak, they would, if challenged, point out that they had no ill-feeling towards the lawn and they were not the ones who made it grow on the site where elephant battles happen to be fought . . .

Martin Jay has recently recalled from semi-oblivion the blunt verdict pronounced by George Orwell in his seminal essay on politics and the English language:

> In our time political speech and writing are largely the defence of the indefensible . . . Political language – and with variations this is true of all political parties, from Conservatives to Anarchists – is designed to make lies sound truthful and murder respectable, and to give an appearance of solidity to pure wind.[1]

Having scrutinized the state of political discourse half a century later, Jay himself could no longer treat 'spin, exaggeration, evasion, half-truths and the like' as a temporary ailment that can be cured, or as an alien intrusion in the struggle for power that with due effort could be replaced by 'straightforward speaking from heart':

> rather than seeing the Big Lie of totalitarian politics as met by the perfect truth sought in liberal democratic ones, a truth based on that quest for transparency and clarity in language we have seen

endorsed by Orwell and his earnest followers, we would be better advised to see politics as the endless struggle between lots of half-truths, cunning omissions, and competing narratives, which may offset each other, but never entirely produce a single consensus.[2]

There is surely a 'cunning omission', or two, in the newspeak phrase 'collateral casualties' or 'collateral damage'. What has been shrewdly omitted is the fact that the 'casualties', whether 'collateral' or not, have been the effect of the way the blow was planned and delivered, since those who planned and delivered it did not particularly care whether the damage spilled over the assumed boundary of the proper target into the hazy (since they kept it out of focus) area of side-effects and unanticipated consequences. There may be a half-truth, if not a downright lie, as well: from the perspective of the declared objective of action, some of its victims may indeed be classified as 'collateral', but it won't be easy to prove that the official and explicit narrative has not been 'economical with truth'; that it indeed tells, as it insists it does, the truth, the whole truth and nothing but the truth about the thoughts and motives nesting in the planners' minds or debated at the planners' meetings. One is entitled to suspect that (to use Robert Merton's distinction between the 'manifest' and 'latent' functions of routine behavioural patterns and particular undertakings) what is 'latent' in this case does not necessarily mean 'unconscious' or 'unwanted'; it may mean instead 'kept secret' or 'covered up'. And mindful of Martin Jay's warning about the apparently irreducible multitude of narratives, we should rather abandon hope of verifying or refuting one or other interpretation 'beyond reasonable doubt'.

It has been the *political* lie, a lie deployed in the service of an explicitly *political* power struggle and of *political* efficiency, that has been the focus of our attention thus far. But 'collateral damage' is a concept in no way confined to the specifically political arena; neither are the 'cunning omissions' and 'half-truths' endemic in it. Power struggles are not conducted solely by professional politicians; and it is not just politicians who are professionally engaged in the search for efficiency. The way in which the dominant narratives, or narratives aspiring to domination, draw the line separating a 'purposeful action' from the action's 'unanticipated consequences' is also a principal stake in the promotion of *economic* interests and in the effort to enhance competitive advantage in the struggle for economic profits.

I suggest that the paramount (though by no means the only) 'collateral damage' perpetrated by that promotion and struggle is an overall and comprehensive commoditization of human life.

In the words of J. Livingstone, 'the commodity form penetrates and reshapes dimensions of social life hitherto exempt from its logic to the point where subjectivity itself becomes a commodity to be bought and sold in the market as beauty, cleanliness, sincerity and autonomy.'[3] And as Colin Campbell puts it – the activity of consuming

> has become a kind of template or model for the way in which citizens of contemporary Western societies have come to view all their activities. Since ... more and more areas of contemporary society have become assimilated to a 'consumer model' it is perhaps hardly surprising that the underlying metaphysics of consumerism has in the process become a kind of default philosophy for all modern life.[4]

Arlie Russell Hochschild encapsulates the most seminal 'collateral damage' perpetrated in the course of the consumerist invasion in a phrase as poignant as it is succinct: 'materialization of love'.

> Consumerism acts to maintain the emotional reversal of work and family. Exposed to a continual bombardment of advertisements through a daily average of three hours of television (half of all their leisure time), workers are persuaded to 'need' more things. To buy what they now need, they need money. To earn money, they work longer hours. Being away from home so many hours, they make up for their absence at home with gifts that cost money. They materialize love. And so the cycle continues.[5]

We may add that their new spiritual detachment and physical absence from the home scene make male and female workers alike impatient with the conflicts, large, small or downright tiny and trifling, which mixing together under one roof inevitably entails.

As the skills needed to converse and seek understanding dwindle, what used to be a challenge to be confronted point blank and then coped with turns increasingly into a pretext for breaking off communication, for escaping and burning bridges behind you. Busy earning more for things they feel they need for happiness, men and women have less time for mutual empathy and for intense, sometimes tortuous and painful, but always lengthy and energy-consuming negotiations, let alone for a reso-lution of their mutual misunderstandings and disagreements. This sets in motion another vicious circle: the better they succeed in 'materializing' their love relationship (as the continuous flow of advertising messages prompts them to do), the fewer opportu-nities are left for the mutually sympathetic understanding called for by the notorious power/care ambiguity of love. Family members are tempted to avoid confrontation and seek respite (or better still a permanent shelter) from domestic infighting; and then the urge to 'materialize' love and loving care acquires yet more impetus, as the more time-consuming and energy-consuming alternatives become ever less attainable at a time when they are more and more needed because of the steadily growing number of points of contention, grudges to be placated and disa-greements clamouring for resolution.

While highly qualified professionals, the apples of company directors' eyes, may all too often be offered in their place of work an agreeable substitute for the cosy homeliness badly missing at home (as Hochschild notes, for them the traditional division of roles between workplace and family homestead tends to be reversed), nothing is offered to employees who are lower in rank, less skilled, and easily replaceable. If some companies, notably Amerco, investigated by Hochschild in depth, 'offer the old *social-ist utopia* to an *elite* of knowledge workers in the top tier of an increasingly divided labour market, other companies may increas-ingly be offering *the worst of early capitalism* to *semiskilled and unskilled workers*'. For the latter, 'neither a kin network nor work associates provide emotional anchors for the individual but rather a gang, fellow drinkers on the corner, or other groups of this sort'.

The search for individual pleasures articulated by the commodi-ties currently offered, a search guided and constantly redirected and refocused by successive advertising campaigns, provides the sole acceptable – indeed badly needed and welcome – substitute for both the uplifting solidarity of workmates and the glowing warmth of caring for and being cared for by nearest and dearest inside the family home and its immediate neighbourhood.

Politicians who call for the resuscitation of dying or terminally ill 'family values', and serious about what their calls imply, should begin by thinking hard about the consumerist roots of the simultaneous wilting of social solidarity inside workplaces and fading of the caring–sharing impulse inside family homes. Just as politicians who call on their voters to show reciprocal respect and who are serious about what their appeal implies ought to think hard about the innate tendency of a society of consumers to instil in their members a willingness to accord other people the same – and no more – respect as they are trained to feel and to show to consumer goods, the objects designed and destined for instantaneous, and possibly untroubled satisfaction, with no strings attached.

Collateral damage left along the track of the triumphant progress of consumerism is scattered all over the social spectre of contemporary 'developed' societies. There is, however, a new category of population, previously absent from the mental maps of social divisions, who can be seen as a collective victim of the 'multiple collateral damage' of consumerism. In recent years, this category has been given the name of the 'underclass'.

The term 'working class', once common but now falling out of use, belonged to the imagery of a society in which the tasks and functions of the better-off and the worse-off were different, and in crucial aspects opposite, but *complementary*. That concept evoked an image of a class of people who have an indispensable role all their own to play in the life of a society; people who make a useful contribution to that society as a whole and expect to be rewarded accordingly. The term 'lower class', then also common though now shunned, was different in belonging to the imagery of a socially mobile society, in which people were on the move and each position was only momentary and in principle amenable to change. That term evoked an image of a class of people who stand, or have been cast, at the bottom of a ladder which they may be able to climb (with effort and luck) to escape from their present inferiority.

The term 'underclass', however, belongs to a completely different image of society: it implies a society that is anything but hospitable and accommodating to all, a society mindful instead of

Carl Schmitt's reminder that the defining mark of sovereignty is the prerogative to *exempt* and *exclude*, and to set aside a category of people to whom the law is applied by *denying* or *withdrawing* its application. The 'underclass' evokes an image of an aggregate of people who have been declared off-limits in relation to *all* classes and the *class hierarchy itself*, with little chance and no need of readmission: people without a role, making no useful contribution to the lives of the rest, and in principle beyond redemption. People who in a class-divided society form no class of their own, but feed on the life juices of all other classes, thereby eroding the class-based order of society; just as in the Nazi imagery of a race-divided human species, Jews were not charged with being another, hostile race, but with being a 'no-race race', a parasite on the body of all other 'right and proper' races, an erosive force diluting the identity and integrity of all races and so sapping and undermining the race-based order of the universe.

Let me add that the term 'underclass' has been exquisitely well chosen. It evokes and enlists associations with the 'underworld', Hades, Sheol, those deeply entrenched primal archetypes of the netherworld, that murky, damp, musty and formless darkness that envelops those who wander away from the well-ordered and meaning-saturated land of the living . . .

Individuals summarily exiled to the 'underclass' can by no stretch of the imagination be visualized as forming a meaningful, integrated 'totality'. They can only be filed and listed together thanks to the alleged similarities in their conduct. The inventory of people crowded together in the generic image of the underclass, as described by Herbert J. Gans, strikes the reader above all by its bewildering variegation:

> This behavioural definition denominates poor people who drop out of school, do not work, and, if they are young women, have babies without benefit of marriage and go on welfare. The behavioural underclass also includes the homeless, beggars, and panhandlers, poor addicts to alcohol and drugs, and street criminals. Because the term is flexible, poor people who live in 'the projects', illegal immigrants, and teenage gang members are often also assigned to the underclass. Indeed, the very flexibility of the behavioural definition is what lends itself to the term becoming a label that can be used to stigmatize poor people, whatever their actual behaviour.[6]

An utterly heterogeneous and extremely variegated collection indeed. What could give at least an appearance of sense to the act of putting them all together? What do single mothers have in common with alcoholics, or illegal immigrants with school dropouts?

One trait that does mark them all is that other people, those who write the list and the list's prospective readers, see no good reason for their existence and imagine that they themselves would be much better off if they weren't around. People are cast in the underclass because they are seen as totally useless; as a nuisance pure and simple, something the rest of us could do nicely without. In a society of consumers – a world that evaluates anyone and anything by their commodity value – they are people with no market value; they are the uncommoditized men and women, and their failure to obtain the status of proper commodity coincides with (indeed, stems from) their failure to engage in a fully fledged consumer activity. They are *failed consumers*, walking symbols of the disasters awaiting fallen consumers, and of the ultimate destiny of anyone failing to acquit herself or himself in the consumer's duties. All in all, they are the 'end is nigh' or the 'memento mori' sandwich men walking the streets to alert or frighten the bona fide consumers. They are the yarn of which nightmares are woven – or, as the official version would rather have it, they are ugly yet greedy weeds, which add nothing to the harmonious beauty of the garden but make the plants famished by sucking out and devouring a lot of the feed.

Since they are all useless, it is the dangers they portend and stand for that dominate the way they are perceived. Everyone else in the society of consumers would gain if *they* vanished. Think: everyone else will gain when *you* fall out of the consumer game and *your* turn to vanish has arrived . . .

'Uselessness' and 'danger' belong to the large family of W. B. Gallie's 'essentially contested concepts'. When they are deployed as tools of designation, they therefore display the flexibility which makes the resulting classifications exceptionally suitable for accommodating all the most sinister demons of the many haunting a society tormented by doubts about the durability of any kind of usefulness, as well as by diffuse, unanchored yet ambient fears. The mental map of the world drawn with their help provides an infinitely vast playground for successive 'moral panics'. The divisions obtained can easily be stretched to absorb and domesticate new threats, while at the same time allowing diffuse terrors to focus on a target which is reassuring just for being specific and tangible.

This is, arguably, a tremendously important use which the uselessness of the underclass offers to a society in which no trade or profession can be certain any longer of its own long-term usefulness and so of its guaranteed market value, and its dangerousness offers a similarly important service, to a society convulsed by anxieties too numerous for it to be able to say with any degree of confidence what there is to be afraid of, and what is to be done to assuage the fear.

All that has been said above does not mean, of course, that there are no beggars, drug-users or unwed mothers, the kinds of miserable and therefore repugnant people referred to as clinching arguments whenever the existence of an underclass is questioned. It does mean, though, that their presence in society does not in the slightest suffice to prove the existence of an 'underclass'. Plunging them all into one category is a decision taken by a filing clerk or his supervisors, not the verdict of 'objective facts'. Collapsing them into one entity, charging them all collectively with parasitism and harbouring malice and unspeakable dangers for the rest of society, is an exercise in *value-laden choice*, not a *description*.

Above all, while the idea of the underclass rests on the presumption that the true society (that is, a totality holding inside it everything necessary to keep it viable) may be smaller than the sum of its parts, the aggregate *denoted* by the name 'underclass' is *bigger* than the sum of its parts: in its case, the act of inclusion adds a new quality which no part on its own would otherwise possess. A 'single mother' and an 'underclass woman' are *not* the same. It takes a great deal of effort (though little thought) to recycle the first into the second.

Contemporary society engages its members primarily as consumers; only secondarily, and in part, does it engage them as producers. To meet the standards of normality, to be acknowledged as a fully fledged, right and proper member of society, one needs to respond promptly and efficiently to the temptations of the consumer market; one needs to contribute regularly to the 'demand

that clears supply', while in times of economic turndown or stagnation being party to the 'consumer-led recovery'. All this the
poor and indolent, people lacking a decent income, credit cards
and the prospect of better days, are not fit to do. Accordingly, the
norm broken by the poor of today, the norm the breaking of which
sets them apart and labels them as 'abnormal', is the norm of
consumer competence or *aptitude*, not that of *employment*.

First and foremost, the poor of today (that is, people who are
'problems' for the rest) are 'non-consumers', not 'unemployed'.
They are defined in the first place through being flawed consumers, since the most crucial of the social duties which they do not
fulfil is that of being active and effective buyers of the goods and
services the market offers. In the account books of a consumer
society, the poor are unequivocally a liability, and by no stretch
of imagination can they be recorded on the side of present or
future assets.

Recast as collateral casualties of *consumerism*, the poor are
now and for the first time in recorded history purely and simply
a worry and a nuisance. They have no merits to relieve, let alone
redeem, their vices. They have nothing to offer in exchange for
the taxpayers' outlays. Money transferred to them is a bad investment, unlikely to be repaid, let alone to bring profit. They form
a black hole that sucks in whatever comes near and spits back
nothing except vague but dark premonitions and trouble.

The poor of the society of consumers are totally useless. Decent
and normal members of society – bona fide consumers – want
nothing from them and expect nothing. No one (most importantly, no one who truly counts, speaks up and is listened to
and heard) needs them. For them, zero tolerance. Society would
be much better off if the poor burnt their tents and allowed
themselves to be burned with them – or just left. The world
would be that much more endearing and pleasant to inhabit
without them inside it. The poor are not *needed*, and so they
are *unwanted*.

The sufferings of the contemporary poor, the poor of the society
of consumers, do not add up to a common cause. Each flawed
consumer licks his or her wounds in solitude, at best in the
company of their as yet unbroken family. Flawed consumers are
lonely, and when they are left lonely for a long time they tend to
become loners; they do not see how society or any social group

(except a criminal gang) can help, they do not hope to be helped, they do not believe that their lot can be changed by any legal means save a lottery win.

Unneeded, unwanted, forsaken – where is their place? The briefest of answers is: out of sight. First, they need to be removed from the streets and other public places used by us, the legitimate residents of the brave consumerist world. If they happen to be fresh arrivals and have their residence permits in less than perfect order, they can be deported beyond boundaries, and so evicted physically from the realm of obligations due to the bearers of human rights. If an excuse for deportation cannot be found, they may still be incarcerated in faraway prisons or prison-like camps, best of all in the likes of the Arizona desert, on ships anchored far from sailing routes, or in high-tech, fully automated jails where they see no one and where no one, even a prison guard, is likely to meet them face to face very often.

To make the physical isolation foolproof, it can be reinforced by mental separation, resulting in the poor being banished from the universe of moral empathy. While the poor are banished from the streets, they can also be banished from the recognizably *human* community: from the world of *ethical* duties. This is done by rewriting their stories away from the language of deprivation to that of depravity. The poor are portrayed as lax, sinful and devoid of moral standards. The media cheerfully cooperate with the police in presenting to the sensation-greedy public lurid pictures of the 'criminal elements', infested by crime, drugs and sexual promiscuity, who seek shelter in the darkness of their forbidding haunts and mean streets. The poor supply the 'usual suspects' to be rounded up, to the accompaniment of a public hue and cry, whenever a fault in the habitual order is detected and publicly disclosed. And so the point is made that the question of *poverty* is, first and foremost, perhaps solely, a question of *law and order*, and one should respond to it in the way one responds to other kinds of law-breaking.

Exempt from the human community, exempt from the public mind. We know what may follow when this happens. There is a strong temptation to get rid altogether of a phenomenon demoted to the rank of a sheer nuisance, unredeemed, not even mitigated, by any ethical consideration that might be due to a harmed, offended and suffering Other; to wipe out a blot on the landscape, to efface a dirty spot on the otherwise pleasingly pure canvas of an orderly world and normal society.

Alain Finkielkraut reminds us of what might happen when ethical considerations are effectively silenced, empathy extinguished and moral barriers taken away:

> Nazi violence was committed not for the liking of it, but out of duty, not out of sadism but out of virtue, not through pleasure but through a method, not by an unleashing of savage impulses and an abandonment of scruples, but in the name of superior values, with professional competence and with the task to be performed constantly in view.[7]

That violence was committed, let me add, amidst a deafening silence from people who thought themselves to be decent and ethical creatures yet saw no reason why the victims of violence, who long before had ceased to be counted among the members of the *human* family, should be targets of their *moral* empathy and compassion. To paraphrase Gregory Bateson, once the loss of moral community is combined with the advanced technology of tackling whatever is seen as a vexing problem, 'your chance of survival will be that of a snowball in hell'. Once coupled with moral indifference, rational solutions to human problems make an explosive mixture indeed.

Many human beings may perish in the explosion, yet the most salient among the victims is the humanity of those who escape the perdition.

Imagination is notoriously selective. Its selectiveness is guided by experience, and particularly by the discontents it spawns.

Every type of social setting produces its own visions of the dangers that threaten its identity, visions made to the measure of the kind of social order it struggles to achieve or to retain. If the self-definition, simultaneously descriptive and postulative, can be thought of as a photographic replica of the setting, visions of threats tend to be the negatives of those photographs. Or, to put this in psychoanalytical terms, threats are projections of a society's own inner ambivalence, and anxieties born of that ambivalence, about its own ways and means, about the fashion in which that society lives and intends to live.

A society unsure about the survival of its mode of being develops the mentality of a besieged fortress. The enemies who lay siege to its walls are its own, very own 'inner demons': the suppressed, ambient fears which permeate its daily life, its 'normality', yet which, to make the daily reality endurable, must be squashed and squeezed out of the lived-through quotidianity and moulded into an alien body – a tangible enemy with a name attached, an enemy one can fight, and fight again, and even hope to conquer.

Such tendencies are ubiquitous and constant, not a specificity of the present-day, liquid modern society of consumers. The novelty, however, will become evident once we recall that the danger which haunted the 'classic', order-building and order-obsessed modern state presiding over the society of producers and soldiers was that of *revolution*. The enemies were the revolutionaries, or, rather, the 'hot-headed, hare-brained, all-too-radical reformists', the subversive forces trying to replace the extant state-managed order with another state-managed order, a counter-order reversing each and every principle by which the present order lived or aimed to live. As the self-image of an orderly, properly functioning society has changed since those times, so also has the image of the threat acquired a fully new shape.

What has been registered in recent decades as rising criminality (a process, let us note, which happened to run parallel to the falling membership of the Communist or other radical, 'subversive' parties of the 'alternative order') is not a product of malfunction or neglect, but consumer society's own product, logically (if not legally) legitimate. What is more, it is also its inescapable product, even if it doesn't qualify as such according to the authority of any official quality commissions. The higher consumer demand is (that is, the more effective is the market seduction of prospective customers), the more safe and prosperous is the consumer society – while, simultaneously, the wider and deeper the gap becomes between those who desire and are *able* to satisfy their desires (those who have been seduced and proceed to act in the way in which the state of being seduced prompts them to act), and those who have been properly seduced but are *unable* to act in the way the properly seduced are expected to act. Truthfully praised as a great equalizer, market seduction is also a uniquely and incomparably effective divider.

One of the features of consumer society most widely commented on is the elevation of novelty and the degradation of routine. Consumer markets excel in dismantling extant routines and pre-empting the planting and entrenchment of new ones – except for the brief timespan needed to empty the warehouses of the implements designed to service them. The same markets, however, attain a yet deeper effect: for the properly trained members of the society of consumers, all and any routine and everything associated with routine behaviour (monotony, repetitiveness) become unbearable; indeed, unliveable. 'Boredom', the absence or even temporary interruption of the perpetual flow of attention-drawing, exciting novelties, turns into a resented and feared bugbear of the consumer society.

To be effective, the enticement to consume, and to consume more, must be transmitted in all directions and addressed indiscriminately to everybody who will listen. But more people can listen than can respond in the fashion intended by the seductive message. Those who cannot act on the desires so induced are treated daily to the dazzling spectacle of those who can. Lavish consumption, they are told, is the sign of success, a highway leading straight to public applause and fame. They also learn that possessing and consuming certain objects and practising certain lifestyles are the necessary condition for happiness; and since 'being happy', as if belatedly following Samuel Butler's premonitions, has become the mark of human decency and entitlement to human respect, it tends also to become the necessary condition of human dignity and self-esteem. 'Being bored', in addition to making one feel uncomfortable, is thereby turning into a shameful stigma, a testimony of negligence or defeat which may lead to a state of acute depression as much as to socio- and psychopathic aggressiveness. To quote Richard Sennett's recent observation, 'with regard to anti-social behaviour I think this is a real problem for poor people . . .', especially perhaps for the 'poor adolescents who are in the grey zone between where they could tip over into being criminals or not'. 'The tipping point' has a lot to do 'with things like boredom, having something to do, having something to belong to . . .'.[8]

If the privilege of 'never being bored' is the measure of a successful life, of happiness and even of human decency, and if intense consumer activity is the prime, royal road to victory over boredom, then the lid has been taken off human desires; no amount of gratifying acquisitions and enticing sensations is likely ever to bring satisfaction in the way once promised by 'keeping up to standards'. There are now no standards to keep up to – or rather no standards which, once reached, can authoritatively endorse the right to acceptance and respect, and guarantee their long duration. The finishing line moves on together with the runner, the goals stay forever a step or two ahead. Records keep being broken, and there seems to be no end to what a human being may desire. 'Acceptance' (the absence of which, let's recall, Pierre Bourdieu defined as the worst of all conceivable kinds of deprivation) is ever more difficult to attain and yet more difficult, nay impossible, to be felt as lasting and secure.

In the absence of unshakeable authorities, people tend to look for guidance to the personal examples currently celebrated. When they do that, however, dazzled and baffled people learn that in the newly privatized ('outsourced', 'contracted out') and thus 'liberated' companies, which they can still remember as hard-up and austere public institutions constantly starved of cash, the present managers draw salaries measured in millions, while those sacked for ineptitude from their managerial chairs are indemnified and compensated, again in millions of pounds, dollars or euros, for their botched and sloppy work. From everywhere, through all communication channels, the message comes loud and clear: there are no precepts except that of grabbing more, and no rules, except the imperative of 'playing your cards right'. But if winning is the sole object of the game, those who get poor hands deal after deal are tempted to opt for a different game where they can reach for other resources, whatever they can muster.

From the point of view of the casino owners, some resources – those they themselves allocate or circulate – are legal tender; all other resources, and particularly those beyond their control, are prohibited. The line dividing the fair from the unfair does not look the same, however, from the point of view of the players, particularly from the point of view of would-be, aspiring players, and most particularly from the point of view of poorly provided aspiring players, who have no access or only limited access to legal tender. They may resort to the resources they *do* have, whether recognized as legal or declared illegal, or opt out of the game altogether – though market seduction has made the latter move all but impossible to contemplate.

The disarming, disempowering and suppressing of hapless and/ or failed players is therefore an indispensable supplement to integration through seduction in a market-led society of consumers. Impotent, indolent players are to be kept out of the game. They are the waste product of the game, a waste product which the game has to go on sedimenting if it is not to grind to a halt and call in the receivers. Were the sedimentation of waste to stop or even be mitigated, the players wouldn't be shown the horrifying sight of the alternative (the only one, they are told) to staying in the game. Such sights are indispensable in order to make them able and willing to endure the hardships and the tensions gestated by lives lived in the game – and they need to be shown repeatedly if awareness of how awesome the penalties for slackness and neglect tend to be is to be continually refreshed and reinforced, and so also the players' willingness to go on with the game.

Given the nature of the game now being played, the misery of those left out of it, once treated as a *collectively caused* blight which needed to be dealt with and *cured by collective means*, has to be reinterpreted as proof of an *individually* committed sin or crime. The dangerous (because potentially rebellious) *classes* are thereby redefined as collections of dangerous (because potentially criminal) *individuals*. Prisons now deputize for the phased-out and fading welfare institutions, and in all probability will have to go on readjusting to the performance of this new function as welfare provisions continue to be thinned out.

To make the prospects bleaker still, the growing incidence of conduct classified as criminal is not an obstacle on the road to a fully fledged and all-embracing consumerist society; it is, on the contrary, its natural and perhaps indispensable accompaniment and prerequisite. This is for a number of reasons, but the main reason among them is perhaps the fact that those left out of the game (the flawed consumers, whose resources do not measure up to their desires, and who therefore have little or no chance of winning if they play the game by its official rules) are the living incarnations of the 'inner demons' specific to consumer life. Their ghettoization and criminalization, the severity of the sufferings administered to them and the overall cruelty of the fate visited on

them are – metaphorically speaking – the princip.
cizing these inner demons and burning them awa)
criminalized margins serve as *soi-disant* tools of .
sewers into which the inevitable but poisonous efl
sumerist seduction are drained off, so that the people
to stay in the game of consumerism need not worr, ⌐ut the
state of their own health.

If this is, however, the prime stimulus of the present exuberance
of what the great Norwegian criminologist Nils Christie called
'the prison industry',[9] then the hope that the process can be
slowed down, let alone halted or reversed in a thoroughly deregulated and privatized society animated and run by the consumer
market, is – to say the least – slight.

The concept of the 'underclass' was coined and first used by
Gunnar Myrdal in 1963, to signal the dangers of deindustrializa-
tion, which he feared likely to render a growing fraction of the
population permanently unemployed and unemployable – not
because of deficiencies or moral faults in the people who found
themselves out of work, but purely and simply because of the lack
of employment for all those who needed it, desired it and were
able to undertake it.

In Myrdal's view, the imminent arrival of what would later be
called 'structural unemployment', and so also of an 'underclass',
would not be the result of the failure of the work ethic to inspire
the living, but of society's failure to guarantee conditions under
which the kind of life the work ethic recommended and inspired
could be lived.[10] The coming 'underclass' in Myrdal's sense of the
word was to consist of the victims of *exclusion* from productive
activity, to be a collective product of *economic* logic, a logic over
which the parts of the population earmarked for exclusion had
no control and little if any influence.

Myrdal's hypothesis was not paid much public attention,
however, while his premonitions were all but forgotten. When
much later, on 29 August 1977, the idea of the 'underclass' was
presented to the public again, via a cover story in *Time* magazine,
it was injected with a significantly altered sense: that of 'a large
group of people who are more intractable, more socially alien and
more hostile than almost anyone had imagined. They are the
unreachables: the American underclass.' A long and continually

expanded list of all sorts of categories followed this definition. It included juvenile delinquents, school dropouts, drug addicts, 'welfare mothers', looters, arsonists, violent criminals, unmarried mothers, pimps, pushers, panhandlers: a roll-call of the inner demons of a well-off, comfortable, pleasure and happiness seeking society – the names of the overt fears of its members and the hidden burdens of their consciences.

'Intractable'. 'Alien'. 'Hostile'. And, as a result of all this, *unreachable*. No point in stretching out a helping hand: it would simply hang in the void, or – worse still – be bitten. Those people are beyond cure; and they are beyond cure because they *chose* a life of disease.

When Ken Auletta undertook a series of exploratory excursions into the 'underclass' world in 1981–2 – reported in the *New Yorker* and later collected in a widely read and highly influential book – he was prompted, or at least so he averred, by the anxiety felt by most of his fellow citizens:

> I wondered: who are those people behind the bulging crime, welfare, and drug statistics – and the all-too-visible rise in antiso-cial behaviour – that afflicts most American cities? . . . I quickly learned that among students of poverty there is little disagreement that a fairly distinct black and white underclass does exist; that this underclass generally feels excluded from society, rejects com-monly accepted values, suffers from *behavioural*, as well as *income* deficiencies. They don't just tend to be poor; to most Americans their behaviour seems aberrant.[11]

Note the vocabulary, the syntax, and the rhetoric of the discourse within which the image of the underclass was generated and settled. Auletta's text is perhaps the best place to study them, because unlike most of his less scrupulous successors Auletta was cautious not to justify a charge of simple 'underclass bashing'; he leant over backwards to manifest his objectivity and to show that he pitied as much as censured the negative heroes of his story.[12]

Note first that the 'bulging crime' and 'bulging welfare' and 'welfare and drug' statistics are mentioned in one breath and set at the same level before the narrative and the argument starts. No argument, let alone proof, was presumed to be needed, let alone offered, to explain why the two phenomena found themselves in each other's company and why they have been classed as instances of the same 'antisocial' behaviour. There was no attempt even to argue explicitly that drug-pushing and living on social welfare are antisocial phenomena of a similar order.

Note as well that in Auletta's description (and those of his numerous followers'), people in the underclass *reject* common values, but they only *feel* excluded. Joining the underclass is an *active* and action-generating initiative, a deliberate step to take one side in the two-sided relationship in which 'most Americans' find themselves on the other, receiving end: that of a *passive*, victimized and suffering target. Were it not for the antisocial mentality and hostile deeds of the underclass, there would be no public trial, just as there would have been no case to ponder, no crime to punish and no negligence to repair.

The rhetoric was followed by practice, which supplied its retrospective 'empirical proof' and from which arguments were drawn which the rhetoric itself had failed to provide. The more numerous and widespread practices became, the more self-evident the diagnoses which triggered them seemed, and the less was the chance that the rhetorical subterfuge would ever be spotted, let alone unmasked and refuted.

Most of Auletta's empirical material was drawn from the Wildcat Skills Training Centre, an institution established with the noble intention of rehabilitating and restoring to society the individuals accused of falling out with the values cherished by society, or rather of putting themselves beyond its boundary. Who was eligible for admission to the centre? A candidate had to be a fairly recent prison convict; or an ex-addict still undergoing treatment; or a female on welfare, without children under the age of six; or a youth between seventeen and twenty who had dropped out of school. Whoever set the rules of admission must have decided beforehand that such 'types', so *distinct* to an untrained eye, suffered from *the same* kind of problem, or rather *presented* society with the same kind of problem – and therefore needed, and were eligible for, *the same* kind of treatment. But what started as a rule-setters' decision turned into reality for the Wildcat Centre inmates: for a considerable time they were put in each other's company, subjected to the same regime, and daily drilled into an acceptance of the commonality of their fate. Being insiders of the Wildcat Centre was, for the duration, all the social identity they needed and all they could reasonably work to obtain. Once more an audacious thesis turned into a self-fulfilling prophecy thanks to the actions it had triggered; once more a word had become flesh.

Auletta was at pains to remind his readers time and again that the condition of 'underclassness' was *not* a matter of poverty, or at least couldn't be explained *solely* by it. He pointed out that if 25 to 29 million Americans lived below the poverty line, only an 'estimated 9 million did not assimilate' and 'operated outside the generally accepted boundaries of society', set apart as they were 'by their "deviant" or antisocial behaviour'.[13] The implicit suggestion was that the elimination of *poverty*, were it at all conceivable, would not put an end to the underclass phenomenon. If one can be poor and yet 'operate within accepted boundaries', then poverty can't be blamed and factors other than poverty must be responsible for descending into the underclass. These factors were seen to be thoroughly subjective, individual afflictions – psychological and behavioural – more often to be found among those living in poverty, perhaps, but not determined by it.

Let me repeat: according to those suggestions, descent into the underclass was a matter of choice; a direct choice in the case of an open challenge to social norms, or an oblique choice deriving from an inattention to norms or from not obeying them zealously enough. Underclass status was a choice, even if a person fell into the underclass simply because he or she had failed to do, or was too lazy to do, what they could and were obliged and expected to do in order to stave off the fall. Choosing not to do what was needed to attain certain goals, in a country of free choosers, is almost automatically, without a second thought, interpreted as choosing *something else* instead; in the case of the underclass, the *unsocial* behaviour was chosen. Falling into the underclass was an *exercise in freedom* . . . In a society of free consumers, curbing one's freedom is impermissible; but it was equally impermissible to refrain from denying or curtailing the freedom of those who would use their liberty to curtail other people's freedoms, by begging, pestering or threatening, by spoiling their fun and burdening their consciences and otherwise making the lives of other people uncomfortable.

The decision to separate the 'problem of the underclass' from the 'issue of poverty' hit several birds with one stone. Its most obvious effect, in a society famous for its beliefs in litigation and compensation, was to deny the people assigned to the underclass the right to press charges and 'claim damages' by presenting themselves as victims (even simply 'collateral' victims) of societal malfunction or wrongdoing. In any litigation that might follow their case, the burden of proof would be shifted fairly and squarely on to the plaintiffs. They were the ones who would have to shoulder the burden of proof – demonstrate their goodwill and determination to be 'like all the rest of us'. Whatever needed to be done would have to be done, at least to start with, by the 'underclassers' themselves (though, of course, there was never a shortage of appointed supervisors and self-appointed legally trained counsellors to advise them as to what it was exactly that they were expected to do). If nothing happened and the spectre of the underclass refused to vanish, the explanation was simple. It was also clear who was to blame. If the rest of society had something to reproach itself for, it was only for its insufficient determination to curtail the iniquitous choices of the 'underclassers' and limit the damage they caused. More police, more prisons, ever more severe, painful and feared punishments then seemed the most obvious means to repair the mistake.

Perhaps more seminal yet was another effect: the *abnormality* of the underclass *normalized* the presence of poverty. It was the underclass that was placed outside the accepted boundaries of society, but the underclass was, as we remember, only a fraction of the 'officially poor'. It is precisely because the underclass was named as the truly big and urgent problem that the bulk of people living in poverty were not a great enough issue that it would need to be tackled urgently. Against the background of the uniformly ugly and repulsive landscape of the underclass, the 'merely poor' (the 'decent poor') shone out as people who – unlike the 'underclassers' – would eventually make all the *right* choices themselves and find their way back into the accepted boundaries of society. Just as falling into the underclass and staying there was a matter of choice, so rehabilitation from the state of poverty was also a choice – the right choice this time. The tacit suggestion conveyed by the idea that the descent of a poor person into the underclass is the outcome of choice is that another choice might accomplish the opposite and lift the poor out of their social degradation.

A central and largely uncontested, since unwritten, rule of a consumer society is that being free to choose requires competence: the knowledge, skills and determination to use the power of choice.

The freedom to choose does not mean that all choices are right – choices can be good and bad, better and worse. The kind of choice eventually made is the evidence of competence or its lack. The 'underclass' of the society of consumers, 'flawed consumers', is presumed to be an aggregate composed of the individual victims of wrong individual choices, and taken to be tangible proof of the personal nature of life's catastrophes and defeats, always an outcome of incompetent personal choices.

In his highly influential tract on the roots of present-day poverty, Lawrence C. Mead singled out the incompetence of individual actors as the paramount cause of the persistence of poverty amid affluence, and of the sordid failure of all the successive policies of the state to eliminate it.[14] Purely and simply, the poor lack the competence to appreciate the advantages of work-followed-by-consumption; they make wrong choices, putting 'nowork' above work, and so cutting themselves off from the delights of bona fide consumers. It is because of that incompetence, says Mead, that the invocation of the work ethic (and obliquely yet inevitably, also of the allures of consumerism) falls on deaf ears and fails to influence the choices of the poor.

The issue therefore, so the story goes, hinges on whether the needy can be responsible for themselves, and, above all, on whether they have the competence to manage their lives. Whatever external, supra-individual causes might be cited, a mystery remains at the heart of 'nowork' – the deliberate, *actively* chosen *passivity* of the seriously poor, their failure to seize the opportunities which the others, normal people like us, willingly embrace. 'To explain nowork,' says Mead, 'I see no avoiding some appeal to psychology or culture. Mostly, seriously poor adults appear to avoid work, not because of their economic situation, but because of what they believe . . .' 'Psychology is the last frontier in the search for the causes of low work effort . . . Why do the poor not seize [the opportunities] as assiduously as the culture assumes they will? *Who exactly are they?*' . . . 'The core of the culture of poverty seems to be inability to control one's life – what psychologists call inefficacy.' The opportunities are there; are not all of us walking proof of that? But opportunities must also be seen for what they are, namely opportunities to be embraced, chances one refuses only at one's own peril – and that takes competence: some wits, some will, and some effort. The poor, the 'failed consumers', obviously lack all three.

Readers of Mead will welcome the news as, all things considered, good, reassuring news: *we* are decent, responsible people, we offer the poor opportunities – whereas *they* are irresponsible, they indecently refuse to take them. Just as doctors reluctantly throw in the towel when their patients consistently refuse to cooperate with the prescribed treatment, so it is our turn to give up our efforts to awake the flawed consumers from their slumber in the face of the stubborn reluctance of the poor to open themselves up to the challenges, but also the rewards and joys, of the consumer life.

It may be shown, though, that the 'psychological factors' may act in precisely the opposite way; that the failure of the 'flawed consumers' to join in the society of consumers as legitimate members results from causes quite opposite to their alleged decision of 'non-participation'. In addition to living in poverty, or at least below the required level of affluence, people classified as the 'underclass' are condemned to social exclusion and deemed ineligible for membership of a society that requires its members to play the consumerist game by the rule precisely because they are, just like the well-off and the rich, all too open to the power-assisted seductions of consumerism – though, unlike the well-off and the rich, they can't really afford to be seduced. As suggested by the conclusions derived from N. R. Shresta's study (quoted by Russell W. Belk),

> the poor are forced into a situation in which they either have to spend what little money or resources they have in senseless consumer objects rather than basic necessities in order to deflect total social humiliation or face the prospect of being teased and laughed at.[15]

Heads you lose, tails they win. For the poor of the society of consumers, not embracing the consumerist model of life means stigma and exclusion, while embracing it portends more of the poverty that bars admission . . .

'As the need for public services has increased, American voters have come to favour reducing the supply of care that government provides, and many favour turning to the beleaguered family as a main source of care,' notes Hochschild.[16] But they found themselves falling out of the frying pan into the fire.

The same consumerist pressures that associate the idea of 'care' with an inventory of consumer commodities such as 'orange juice, milk, frozen pizza and microwave ovens' strip the families of their social-ethical skills and resources, and disarm them in their uphill struggle to cope with the new challenges; challenges aided and abetted by the legislators, who attempt to reduce state financial deficits through the expansion of the 'care deficit' ('cutting funds for single mothers, the disabled, the mentally ill, and the elderly').

A state is 'social' when it promotes the principle of *communally endorsed*, collective insurance against individual misfortune and its consequences. It is primarily that principle – declared, set in operation and trusted to be in working order – that recast the otherwise abstract idea of 'society' into the experience of felt and lived community through replacing the 'order of egoism' (to deploy John Dunn's terms), bound to generate an atmosphere of mutual mistrust and suspicion, with the 'order of equality', inspiring confidence and solidarity. It is the same principle which lifts members of society to the status of *citizens*, that is, makes them stakeholders in addition to being stockholders: beneficiaries, but also actors – the wardens as much as the wards of the 'social benefits' system, individuals with an acute interest in the common good understood as a network of shared institutions that can be trusted, and realistically expected, to guarantee the solidity and reliability of the state-issued 'collective insurance policy'.

The application of such a principle may, and often does, protect men and women from the plague of *poverty*; most importantly, however, it can become a profuse *source of solidarity*, able to recycle 'society' into a common good, shared, communally owned and jointly cared for, thanks to the defence it provides against the twin horrors of *misery* and *indignity* – that is, of the terrors of being excluded, of falling or being pushed overboard from the fast-accelerating vehicle of progress, of being condemned to 'social redundancy', denied the respect due to human beings and otherwise designated as 'human waste'.

The 'social state' was to be, in its original intention, an arrangement to serve precisely such purposes. Lord Beveridge, to whom we owe the blueprint for the postwar British 'welfare state', believed that his vision of comprehensive, collectively endorsed insurance for *everyone* was the inevitable consequence or rather indispensable complement of the liberal idea of individual freedom, as well as a necessary condition of *liberal democracy*. Franklin Delano Roosevelt's declaration of war on fear was based on the same assumption. The assumption was reasonable: after all, freedom of choice is bound to come together with uncounted and uncountable risks of failure, and many people will find such risks unbearable, fearing that they may exceed their personal ability to cope. For many people, freedom of choice will remain an elusive phantom and idle dream unless the fear of defeat is mitigated by an insurance policy issued in the name of community, a policy they can trust and rely on in case of personal failure or a freak blow of fate.

If freedom of choice is granted in theory but unattainable in practice, the pain of *hopelessness* will surely be topped with the ignominy of *haplessness* – because the ability to cope with life's challenges tested daily is that very workshop in which the self-confidence of individuals, and so also their sense of human dignity and their self-esteem, are formed or melted away. Besides, without collective insurance there will hardly be much stimulus to political engagement – and certainly not for participation in a democratic ritual of elections, since salvation is unlikely to arrive indeed from a political state that is not, and refuses to be, a *social* state. Without social rights *for all*, a large and in all probability growing number of people will find their political rights useless and unworthy of their attention. If political rights are necessary to set *social* rights in place, social rights are indispensable to keep *political* rights in operation. The two rights need each other for their survival; that survival can only be their joint achievement.

The social state is the ultimate modern embodiment of the idea of community: that is, the institutional incarnation of such an idea in its modern form of an abstract, imagined totality woven of reciprocal dependence, commitment and solidarity. Social rights – rights to respect and dignity – tie that imagined totality to the daily realities of its members and found that imagination in the solid ground of life experience; those rights certify, simultaneously, the veracity and realism of mutual trust *and* of trust in the shared institutional network that endorses and validates collective solidarity.

The sentiment of 'belonging' translates as trust in the benefits of human solidarity, and in the institutions that arise out of that solidarity and promise to serve it and assure its reliability. All those truths were spelled out in the Swedish Social Democratic programme of 2004:

> Everyone is fragile at some point in time. We need each other. We live our lives in the here and now, together with others, caught up in the midst of change. We will all be richer if all of us are allowed to participate and nobody is left out. We will all be stronger if there is security for everybody and not only for a few.

Just as the carrying power of a bridge is not measured by the average strength of its pillars but by the strength of the weakest pillar, and grows together with that strength, the confidence and resourcefulness of a society are measured by the security, resourcefulness and self-confidence of its weakest sections and grow as they grow. Contrary to the assumption of the advocates of the 'third way', social justice and economic efficiency, loyalty to the tradition of the social state and the ability to modernize swiftly (and, most significantly, with little or no damage to social cohesion and solidarity), need not be and are not at loggerheads. On the contrary, as the social democratic practice of the Nordic countries amply demonstrates and confirms, 'the pursuit of a more socially cohesive society is the necessary precondition for modernization by consent.'[17]

Contrary to the grossly premature obituaries scribbled by the promoters and heralds of the 'third way', the Scandinavian pattern is nowadays anything but a relic of the past and of hopes now frustrated, not just a blueprint now dismissed by popular consent as outdated. Just how topical and how alive its underlying principles are, and how strong its chances of inflaming the human imagination and inspiring people to act, is shown by the recent triumphs of the emergent or resurrected social states in Venezuela, Bolivia, Brazil or Chile, gradually yet indefatigably changing the political landscape and the popular mood of the Latin part of the Western hemisphere, bearing all the marks of that 'left hook' with which, as Walter Benjamin pointed out, all truly decisive blows tend to be delivered in human history. However hard it may be to perceive that truth in the daily flow of consumerist routines, this is the truth nevertheless.

To avoid misunderstanding, let it be clear that the 'social state' in the society of consumers is neither intended nor practised as an alternative to the principle of consumer choice – just as it was not meant and did not act as an alternative to the 'work ethic' in the society of producers. The countries with firmly established principles and institutions of a social state happen also to be the countries with impressively high levels of consumption, just as the countries with firmly established principles and institutions of a social state in societies of producers were also the countries whose industry thrived . . .

The meaning of the social state in the society of consumers, just as it was in the society of producers, is to defend society against the 'collateral damage' that the guiding principle of social life would cause if it were not monitored, controlled and constrained. Its purpose is to protect society against multiplying the ranks of the 'collateral victims' of consumerism: the excluded, the outcasts, the underclass. Its task is to salvage human solidarity from erosion and the sentiments of ethical responsibility from fading.

In Britain, the neoliberal assault against the principles of the social state was sold to the nation under Margaret Thatcher's slogan, as if quoted verbatim from the publicity handbook of the consumer market and certain to sound sweet to every consumer's ear: 'I want a doctor of my choice, at the time of my choice.' The Tory governments which followed Margaret Thatcher faithfully followed the pattern she set – as with John Major's 'citizen's charter' that redefined the members of the national community as satisfied customers.

The consolidation of the neoliberal 'order of egoism' was conducted by the 'New Labour' administration under the codename of 'modernization'. As the years went by, few if any objects that had heretofore evaded commoditization escaped the modernizing zeal unscathed. Increasingly, in the face of a dearth of objects still unaffected (that is, areas of life still outside the bounds of the consumer market), yesterday's 'modernized' settings became objects of new rounds of modernization, letting in more private capital and yet more market competition. Rather than being conceived of as a one-off operation, 'modernization' turned into the permanent condition of social and political institutions, further eroding the value of duration, together with the prudence of long-term thinking, and reinforcing the ambience of uncertainty, temporariness and state of 'until further notice' on which consumer commodity markets are known to thrive.

This was, arguably, the greatest service which the activity of government rendered to the cause of the neoliberal revolution and to the uncontested rule of the 'invisible hand' of the market ('invisible' because of eluding all efforts to watch, guess or predict, let alone direct and correct, its moves; a 'hand' which any poker player dreams of, rightly expecting it to be unbeatable). All their particular marks notwithstanding, the successive bouts of modernization made the invisible hand yet more invisible, putting it ever more securely beyond the reach of the available instruments of political, popular and democratic intervention.

A most salient collateral casualty of such governmental activity was, paradoxically (or not that paradoxically after all), the political realm itself, being relentlessly tapered and emaciated through 'subsidiarizing' or 'contracting out' more and more of the functions previously politically directed and administered in favour of explicitly non-political market forces. And as the deregulation and privatization of the economy proceeded at full speed, as nominally state-owned assets were one by one released from political supervision, as personal taxation for collective needs stayed frozen, thereby impoverishing the collectively managed resources required for such needs to be met, the all-explaining and all-excusing incantation of 'there is no alternative' (another legacy of Margaret Thatcher's) unstoppably turned (more correctly, *was* turned) into a self-fulfilling prophecy.

The process has been thoroughly explored and its direction thoroughly documented, so there is little point in restating once more what is public knowledge, or at least has had every chance of becoming public knowledge if attention has been paid. What has been left somewhat out of the focus of public attention, however, while deserving all the attention it can muster, is the role which almost every single 'modernizing' measure has played in the *continuing decomposition and crumbling of social bonds and communal cohesion* – precisely the assets which might enable British men and women to face, confront and tackle the old and new, past and future challenges of the consumerist 'pensée unique'.

Among the many bright and not so bright ideas for which Margaret Thatcher will be remembered was her discovery of the non-existence of society: 'There is no such thing as "society" . . . There are only individuals and families,' she declared. But it took a lot more effort by her and her successors to recast that figment of Thatcher's fanciful imagination into a fairly precise description of the real world, as seen from the *inside* of its inhabitants' experience.

The triumph of rampant, individual and individualizing consumerism over the 'moral economy' and social solidarity was not a foregone conclusion. A society pulverized into solitary individuals and (crumbling) families could not have been built without Thatcher first thoroughly clearing the building site. It could not have been built without her successes in incapacitating the self-defence; associations of those who needed collective defence; in stripping the incapacitated of most of the resources they could use to recover collectively the strength that had been denied to them or lost by them individually; in severely curtailing both the 'self' and the 'government' bits in the practice of local self-government; in making many expressions of disinterested solidarity into a punishable crime; in 'deregulating' factory and office staffs, once greenhouses of social solidarity, into aggregates of mutually suspicious individuals competing in the style of 'each man for himself and the devil take the hindmost', of the *Big Brother* or *The Weakest Link*, or in finishing the job of transforming the universal entitlements of proud citizens into the stigmas of the indolent or outcasts accused of living 'at the taxpayer's expense'. Thatcher's innovations not only survived the years of successive governments – they remained seldom questioned and by and large intact.

What survived as well, and emerged reinforced, were many of Thatcher's innovations in the language of politics. Today, as much as twenty years ago, the vocabulary of British politicians knows of individuals and their families solely as subjects of duties and objects of legitimate concern, while referring to 'communities' mostly as sites where the problems abandoned by the 'great society' at the government's behest need to be tackled in cottage-industry mode (as, for instance, in the context of the mentally disabled dropped by state-run medical care, or in the context of the need to stop the un- or underemployed, undereducated and prospectless youngsters, denied their dignity, from 'tipping over' on to the side of mischief).

And as more and more water flows under the bridges, the world before the Thatcherite revolution is being all but forgotten by older people, while never having been experienced by the young. To those who have forgotten or have never tasted life in that other world, it seems indeed that there is no alternative to the present one . . . or rather, any alternative has become all but unimaginable.

To the acclaim of some enthusiastic observers of the new trends, the void left behind by citizens massively retreating from the extant political battlefields to be reincarnated as consumers is filled by ostentatiously non-partisan and ruggedly unpolitical 'consumer activism'.

The snag, however, is that this sort of replacement does not widen the ranks of 'socially concerned' men and women involved and engaged in public issues (that is, bearing the qualities deemed to be the defining features of citizens of the polis). The new variety of activism engages a smaller part of the electorate than the orthodox political parties – no longer expected, let alone trusted, to represent their voters' interests and so falling out of public favour – can currently manage to mobilize in the heat of election campaigns. And, as Frank Furedi warns, 'Consumer activism thrives in the condition of apathy and social disengagement.' But does it fight back against the spreading political apathy? Does it provide an antidote to the new public indifference to things once considered common and shared causes? It needs to be seen clearly, says Furedi, that

> the consumerist critique of representative democracy is fundamentally an anti-democratic one. It is based on the premise that unelected individuals who possess a lofty moral purpose have a greater right to act on the public's behalf than politicians elected through an imperfect political process. Environmentalist campaigners, who derive their mandate from a self selected network of advocacy groups, represent a far narrower constituency than an elected

politician. Judging by its record, the response of consumer activism to the genuine problem of democratic accountability, is to avoid it altogether in favour of opting for interest group lobbying.[18]

'There is little doubt that the growth of consumer activism is bound up with the decline of traditional forms of political participation and social engagement' is Furedi's verdict based on his thoroughly documented study. What one may doubt, however, is whether it brings about social engagement in a new form – and in a form that can prove as effective in laying the foundations of social solidarity as the 'traditional forms', despite all their well-recorded shortcomings, used to be.

'Consumer activism' is a symptom of the growing disenchantment with politics. To quote Neil Lawson, 'as there is nothing else to fall back on, it is likely that people then give up on the whole notion of collectivism and therefore any sense of a democratic society and fall back on the market (and, let me add, their own consumer skills and activities) as the arbiter of provision.'[19]

The evidence, to be sure, is ambiguous so far. A survey conducted at the start of the 2005 electoral campaign, suggests that 'contrary to popular perception the British public is not apathetic about politics. That is the conclusion of a new report from the Electoral Commission and the Hansard Society, which found that 77 per cent of those polled by MORI were interested in national issues'.[20] It adds right away, however, that 'this high level of basic interest is compared to the minority 27 per cent who feel that they actually have a say in the way the country is run.' Judging from the precedents, one could surmise therefore (and rightly, as the elections that followed the survey have since shown) that the actual number of people eventually going to the electoral booths would fall somewhere between those two figures, landing closer to the lower of the two.

Many more people declare their interest in whatever has been brandished in the front-page headlines of the press or on TV 'news updates' as a 'national issue' than consider it worth their effort of walking to the polling station in order to give their vote to one of the political parties offered for their choice.

Furthermore, since, in a society oversaturated with information, headlines serve mostly (and effectively!) to erase from public memory the headlines of the day before, all the issues recast by the headlines as of 'public interest' have only a meagre chance of surviving from the date of the latest opinion poll to the date of the nearest elections. Most importantly, the two things – the interest in 'national issues' as seen on TV or on the front pages of the dailies, and participation in the extant democratic process – just don't congeal in the minds of the rising number of citizens-turned-consumers in the era of pointillist time. The second, a long-term investment requiring time to mature, does not seem to be a relevant response to the first, another 'infotainment' event with neither roots in the past nor a foothold in the future.

The 'Guardian Student' website of 23 March 2004 gave the information that 'three-quarters (77 per cent) of first-year university students are not interested in taking part in political protests . . . while 67 per cent of freshers believe that student protest isn't effective and doesn't make any difference, according to the Lloyds TSB/Financial Mail on Sunday Student Panel.' It quotes Jenny Little, editor of the student page in the *Financial Mail on Sunday*, as saying: 'Students today must cope with a great deal – the pressure to get a good degree, the need to work part-time to support themselves and to get work experience to ensure that their CVs stand out from the crowd . . . It's not surprising that politics falls to the bottom of the pile of priorities for this generation, though, in real terms, it has never been more important.'

In a study dedicated to the phenomenon of political apathy, Tom DeLuca suggests that the apathy is not an issue in its own right, but 'more a clue about the others, about how free we are, how much power we really have, what we can fairly be held responsible for, whether we are being well served . . . It implies a condition under which one suffers'.[21] Political apathy 'is a state of mind or a political fate brought about by forces, structures, institutions, or elite manipulation over which one has little control and perhaps little knowledge'. DeLuca explores all those factors in depth, to paint a realistic portrait of what he calls 'the second face of political apathy' – the 'first face' being, according to various political scientists, an expression of contentment with the state of affairs or the exercise of the right to free choice, and more generally (as stated in the classic 1954 study *Voting* by Bernard Berelson, Paul Lazarsfeld and William McPhee, later rehashed by Samuel Huntington) a phenomenon 'good for democracy' because of 'making mass democracy work'.

And yet if one wants to decode in full the social realities to which rising political apathy provides a clue and which it signals, one would need to look even beyond the 'second face', which itself, as Tom Deluca rightly claims, has been unduly neglected or only perfunctorily sketched by the mainstream scholars of political science. One would need to recall the earlier meaning of 'democracy' which once made it into a battle cry of the self-same 'deprived and suffering masses' who today turn away from exercising their hard-won electoral rights. They are consumers first, citizens (if at all) a distant second. To really become the first takes a level of constant vigilance and effort that hardly leaves time for the activities for which the second would call.

Filip Remunda and Vit Klusák, students of the Prague film school, financed by the Czech Ministry of Culture, have recently produced and directed 'Czech Dream', a film unlike any other film: a large-scale social experiment rather than a mere documentary, and an exercise in the portrayal of social reality that may well expose the fiction hiding behind the notorious 'reality TV' shows.

Remunda and Klusák announced, in an intense country-wide advertising campaign, the imminent inauguration of a new supermarket. The campaign itself, planned and conducted by a commissioned PR company, was a mastepiece of the marketing art. It started by spreading rumours of an allegedly well-guarded secret: a mysterious, extraordinary temple of consumerism, currently under construction in an undisclosed place, was shortly to be made available to customers. In subsequent stages, the campaign deliberately and successfully disturbed and disrupted the shopping/consumer routine of viewers by calling them to reflect on their daily mundane and monotonous shopping practices and so converting those hitherto unexamined and habitual activities into issues to be thought about. This was done by provoking the 'targets' of the publicity campaign to pause and ponder, and by insinuating through slogans like 'stop spending your money!' or 'do not buy' that the moment to *delay* (how uncommonly!) their gratification had arrived; and then by gradually beefing up curiosity and excitement by leaking ever more appetizing bits of information about the delights awaiting those who agreed to postpone the gratification of their desires until the mysterious brand-new supermarket opened. The supermarket, the company behind it complete with its logo, and the wonders that the company was to offer were all pure inventions of the film-makers. But the excitement and lust they bred were quite real.

On the appointed morning and at the appointed place, finally revealed in hundreds of posters around the town, thousands of consumers gathered ready for action, only to face a long stretch of neglected, overgrown and unmowed lawn with the contours of a colourful, ornate building at its other end. With each of the thousands of eager customers desperate to arrive at the gate before the others, the crowd ran through the damp, gasping for breath – only to reach a painted facade sustained by a huge scaffolding, obviously assembled ad hoc, and hiding nothing but another stretch of similarly unmowed, unattended, overgrown and straggly grass . . .

As if in a flash of soothsayer vision, Günther Anders noted exactly half century ago:

> It seems right to say that nothing defines us, the humans of the present, more than our incapacity to stay mentally 'up to date' regarding the progress of our products, that is to control the rhythm of our own creation and to repossess in the future (which we call our 'present') the instruments which have taken hold of us . . . It is not entirely impossible that we, who fabricate these products, are on the point of creating a world with which we won't be able to keep pace and which will completely exceed our power of 'understanding', our imagination and emotional endurance, as much as it will stay beyond the capacity of our responsibility.[22]

Notes

Introduction

The epigraph is from Pierre Bourdieu, *Pascalian Meditations*, Polity Press, Cambridge, p. 242.

1 See Sean Dodson, 'Show and tell online', *Technology Guardian*, 2 Mar. 2006.
2 See Paul Lewis, 'Teenage networking websites face anti-paedophile investigation', *Guardian*, 3 July 2006.
3 Eugène Enriquez, 'L'idéal type de l'individu hypermoderne: l'individu pervers?', in Nicole Aubert (ed.), *L'Individu hypermoderne*, Erès, 2004, p. 49.
4 See Nick Booth, 'Press 1 if you're poor, 2 if you're loaded . . .', *Guardian*, 2 Mar. 2006.
5 See Alan Travis, 'Immigration shake-up will bar most unskilled workers from outside EU', *Guardian*, 8 Mar. 2006.
6 In an interview published by *Le Monde*, 28 Apr. 2006.
7 Kracauer, *Die Angestellen*, essays first serialized in the *Frankfurter Allgemeine Zeitung* in 1929, and published in book form by Suhrkamp in 1930. Here quoted from Quintin Hoare's translation, Siegfried Kracauer, *The Salaried Masses: Duty and Distraction in Weimar Germany*, Verso, 1998, p. 39.
8 Germaine Greer, *The Future of Feminism*, Dr J. Tans Lecture, Studium Generale Universiteit Maastricht, 2004, p. 13.
9 See Edmund L. Andrews, 'Vague law and hard lobbying add up to billions for big oil', *New York Times*, 27 Mar. 2006.

10 See Arlie Russell Hochschild, *The Time Bind: When Work becomes Home and Home becomes Work*, Henry Holt, 1997, pp. xviii–xix.

11 Don Slater, *Consumer Culture and Modernity*, Polity, 1997, p. 33.

12 Georg Simmel, 'Die Grossstädte und das Geistesleben' (1902–3); here quoted in the translation by Kurt H. Wolff, 'Metropolis and mental life', in *Classic Essays on the Culture of Cities*, ed. Richard Sennett, Appleton-Century-Crofts, 1969, p. 52.

13 See Bryan Gordon's interview, *Observer Magazine*, 21 May 2006, pp. 20–4.

14 See 'Why today's singles are logging on in search for love at first byte', *The Times*, 5 Jan. 2006.

15 Jennie Bristow, 'Are we addicted to love?', at www.spiked-online.com.

16 Josie Appleton, 'Shopping for love', at ibid.

17 See John Keane, 'Late capitalist nights', *Soundings* (Summer 2006), pp. 66–75.

18 Ivan Klima, *Between Security and Insecurity*, Thames and Hudson, 1999, pp. 60–2.

19 See *Consuming Cultures, Global Perspectives*, ed. John Brewer and Frank Trentmann, Berg, 2006.

Chapter 1   Consumerism versus Consumption

1 See Colin Campbell, 'I shop therefore I know that I am: the metaphysical basis of modern consumerism', in *Elusive Consumption*, ed. Karin M. Ekström and Helene Brembeck, Berg, 2004, pp. 27ff.

2 See Max Weber, *Wirtschaft und Gesellschaft*, here quoted after the translation by A. R. Henderson and Talcott Parsons, *The Theory of Social and Economic Organization*, Hodge, 1947, p. 110.

3 Mary Douglas, *In the Active Voice*, Routledge and Kegan Paul, 1988, p. 24.

4 See Slater, *Consumer Culture and Modernity*, p. 100.

5 See Stephen Bertman, *Hyperculture: The Human Cost of Speed*, Praeger, 1998.

6 See Michel Maffesoli, *L'Instant eternel. Le Retour du tragique dans les sociétés postmodernes*, La Table Ronde, 2000, p. 16.

7 See Nicole Aubert, *Le Culte de l'urgence. La Société malade du temps*, Flammarion, 2003, pp. 187, 193.

8 Maffesoli, *L'Instant eternel*, p. 56.

9 Franz Rosenzweig, *Star of Redemption*, trans. William W. Hallo, Routledge and Kegan Paul, 1971, pp. 226–7.

10 See Michael Lövy, *Fire Alarm: Reading Walter Benjamin's 'On the Concept of History'*, Verso, 2005, pp. 102–5.

11 See Walter Benjamin, 'Theses on the concept of history', in *Selected Writings, Volume 4 (1938–1940)*, trans. Edmund Jephcott and others, Harvard University Press, 2003.

12 See Siegfried Kracauer, *History: The Last Things before the Last*, Markus Wiener, 1994, pp. 160–1.

13 Italo Calvino, *Invisible Cities*, trans. William Weaver, Vintage, 1997, p. 114.

14 See 'Is recycling a waste of time?', *Observer Magazine*, 15 Jan. 2006.

15 See Thomas Hylland Eriksen, *Tyranny of the Moment: Fast and Slow Time in the Information Age*, Pluto Press, 2001.

16 See Ignazio Ramonet, *La Tyrannie de la communication*, Galilée, 1999, p. 184.

17 Eriksen, *Tyranny of the Moment*, p. 92.

18 Ibid., p. 17.

19 See Bill Martin, *Listening to the Future: The Time of Progressive Rock 1968–1978*, Feedback, 1997, p. 292.

20 Eriksen, *Tyranny of the Moment*, pp. 109, 113.

21 Georg Simmel, *The Metropolis and Mental Life*, here quoted in Kurt Wolff's translation of 1950, reprinted in *Classic Essays on the Culture of Cities*, ed. Richard Sennett, Appleton-Century-Crofts, 1969, p. 52.

22 Rolland Munro, 'Outside paradise: melancholy and the follies of modernization', *Culture and Organization*, 4 (2005), pp. 275–89.

23 Here quoted after George Monbiot, 'How the harmless wanderer in the woods became a mortal enemy', *Guardian*, 23 Jan. 2006.

24 Thomas Mathiesen, *Silently Silenced: Essays on the Creation of Acquiescence in Modern Society*, Waterside Press, 2004, p. 15.

25 See Zygmunt Bauman, *Individualized Society*, Polity, 2003, and *Liquid Love*, Polity, 2004.

26 Colette Dowling, *Cinderella Complex*, PocketBook, 1991.

27 See Arlie Russell Hochschild, *The Commercialization of Intimate Life*, University of California Press, 2003, pp. 21ff.

28 See Frank Mort, 'Competing domains: democratic subjects and consuming subjects in Britain and the United States since 1945', in *The Making of the Consumer: Knowledge, Power and Identity in the Modern World*, ed. Frank Trentmann, Berg, 2006, pp. 225ff. Mort quotes the Henley Centre's reports *Planning for Social Change* (1986), *Consumer and Leisure Futures* (1997) and *Planning for Consumer Change* (1999).

Chapter 2   Society of Consumers

1 See Frank Trentmann, 'Genealogy of the consumer', in *Consuming Cultures, Global Perspectives*, ed. Brewer and Trentmann, pp. 23ff.

2 See Zygmunt Bauman, *Work, Consumerism and the New Poor*, Open University Press, 2005, ch. 1.

3 Daniel Thomas Cook, 'Beyond either/or', *Journal of Consumer Culture*, 2 (2004), p. 149.

4 Quoted from N. R. Shrestha by Russell W. Belk, 'The human consequences of consumer culture', in *Elusive Consumption*, ed. Karin M. Ekström and Helene Brembeck, Berg, 2004, p. 69.

5 See Günther Anders, *Die Antiquiertheit des Menschen*, vol. 1: *Über die Seele im Zeitalter der zweiten industriellen Revolution*, C. H. Beck, 1956; quoted here after the French edition published by Encyclopédie des Nuisances, 2002, pp. 37ff.

6 Ibid., p. 16.

7 In Decca Aitkenhead, 'Sex now', *Guardian Weekend*, 15 Apr. 2006.

8 Quoted after Anne Perkins, 'Collective failure', *Guardian Work*, 22 Apr. 2006.

9 Daniel Thomas Cook, *The Commodification of Childhood*, Duke University Press, 2004, p. 12.

10 See Aubert, *Le Culte de l'urgence*, pp. 82ff.

11 All the following quotations come from *The Future of an Illusion* and *Civilization and its Discontents*, in James Strachey's edition, The Penguin Freud Library, vol. 12, Penguin, 1991, pp. 179–341.

12 See Richard Rorty, 'The end of Leninism and history as comic frame', in *History and the Idea of Progress,* ed. Arthur R. Melzer, Jerry Weinberger and M. Richard Zinman, Cornell University Press, 1995, p. 216.

13 See Patrick Collinson, 'Study reveals financial crisis of the 18–40s', *Guardian*, 28 Mar. 2006.

14 See Paul Krugman, 'Deep in debt, and denying it', *International Herald Tribune*, 14 Feb. 2006.

Chapter 3   Consumerist Culture

1 Maffesoli, *L'Instant eternal*, pp. 40–1.

2 Douglas, *In the Active Voice*, p. 24.

3 Vincent de Gaulejac, 'Le sujet manqué. L'Individu face aux contradictions de l'hypermodernité', in *L'Individu hypermoderne*, ed. Aubert, p. 134.

4   Ellen Seiter, *Sold Separately: Children and Parents in Consumer Culture.* Rutgers University Press, 1993, p. 3.

5   Aubert, *Le Culte de l'urgence*, pp. 62–3.

6   See Alain Ehrenberg, *La Fatigue d'être soi*, Odile Jacob, 1998.

7   Aubert, *Le Culte de l'urgence*, pp. 107–8.

8   Slater, *Consumer Culture and Modernity*, p. 100.

9   See Lesław Hostyński, *Wartości w świecie konsumpcji.* Wydawnictwo Uniwersytetu Marii Curie-Skłodowskiej, 2006, pp. 108ff.

10 See Pascal Lardellier, 'Rencontres sur internet. L'amour en révolution', in *L'Individu contemporain. Regards sociologiques.* ed. Xavier Molénat, Éditions Sciences Humaines, 2006, p. 229.

11 See Keane, 'Late capitalist nights', pp. 66–75.

12 Eriksen, *Tyranny of the Moment*, pp. 2–3.

13 *Ibid.*, p. vii.

14 Elżbieta Tarkowska, 'Zygmunt Bauman o czasie i procesach temporalizacji', in *Kultura i Społeczeństwo*, 3 (2005), pp. 45–65.

15 See Thomas Frank, *Marché de droit divin. Capitalisme sauvage et populisme de marché*, Agone (Marseille), 2003.

16 See Jodi Dean, 'Communicative capitalism: circulation and the foreclosure of politics', *Cultural Politics* (Mar. 2005), pp. 51–73.

17 See Christopher Lasch, 'The age of limits', in *History and the Idea of Progress,* ed. Arthur M. Melzer, Jerry Weinberger and M. Richard Zinman, Cornell University Press, 1955, p. 240.

18 See Kwame Anthony Appiah, *The Ethics of Identity,* Princeton University Press, 2005.

19 Joseph Brodsky, *On Grief and Reason,* Farrar, Straus and Giroux, 1995, pp. 107–8.

20 Andrzej Stasiuk, *Tekturowy samolot,* Wydawnictwo Czarne, 2000, p. 59.

21 Slawomir Mrozek, *Male listy,* Noir sur Blanc, 2002, p. 123.

22 Kracauer, *History*, p. 148.

23 See Francis Jauréguiberry, 'Hypermodernité et manipulation de soi', in *L'Individu hypermoderne,* ed. Aubert, pp. 158ff.

Chapter 4   Collateral Casualties of Consumerism

1   In George Orwell, *A Collection of Essays*, Harcourt Brace Jovanovich, 1953.

2   See Martin Jay, 'The ambivalent virtues of mendacity', in *Education and the Spirit of Time*, ed. Olli-Pekka Moisio and Juha Suoranta, Sense, 2006, pp. 91ff.

3 See J. Livingstone, 'Modern subjectivity and consumer culture', in *Consuming Desires: Consumption, Culture and the Pursuit of Happiness*, ed. S. Strasser, C. McGovern and M. Judt, Cambridge University Press, 1998, p. 416. Here quoted from Belk, 'The human consequences of consumer culture', p. 71.

4 Campbell, 'I shop therefore I know that I am', pp. 41–2.

5 See Hochschild, *The Commercialization of Intimate Life*, pp. 208ff.

6 H. J. Gans (1995) *The War against the Poor: The Underclass and Antipoverty Policy*, Basic Books, 1995, p. 2.

7 A. Finkielkraut, *L'Humanité perdue. Essai sur le XXe siècle*, Seuil, 1996.

8 See Richard Sennett's interview by Daniel Leighton 'The culture of the new capitalism', *Renewal*, 1 (2006), p. 47.

9 N. Christie, *Crime Control as Industry*, Routledge, 1993.

10 Gunnar Myrdal, *Economic Theory and Underdeveloped Countries*, Duckworth, 1957.

11 K. Auletta, *The Underclass*, Random House, 1982, p. xiii. The language of most current American debate concerning the phenomenon of the underclass is much more in line with the uncompromising rhetoric of Edward Banfield: 'The lower-class individual lives from moment to moment . . . Impulse governs his behavior, either because he cannot discipline himself to sacrifice a present for a future satisfaction or because he has no sense of the future. He is therefore radically improvident; whatever he cannot consume immediately he considers valueless. His taste for "action" takes precedence over anything else' (E. Banfield, *The Unheavenly City: The Nature and Future of our Urban Crisis*, Little, Brown, 1968, pp. 34–5). Let us note that the Banfield diatribe aimed at the 'underclass' sounds like a very accurate description of the 'ideal consumer' in a society of consumers. In this, as in most other discussions, the 'underclass' serves as a dumping ground for the demons haunting the consumer's tormented soul.

12 Auletta's field research brought him too close to the objects of the standardized treatment not to notice how empirically faulty are the generalized labels and wholesale classifications. At the end of his book, which presents one long story of a power-assisted *unification* of the underclass, he states: 'The one great lesson I learned from my reporting among the underclass and the poor is that generalizations – bumper stickers – are the enemies of understanding. It is perilous to generalize about the "lower class" . . . or about "victims" . . . or about poverty being "virtually eliminated" . . . or about government being "the problem". From a height of thirty

thousand feet, everyone and everything looks like an ant' (Auletta, *The Underclass*, p. 317). Expectedly, such warnings went unheeded. In its journalistic, political and popular reception Auletta's study served as another reinforcement of the unified image of the underclass.

13 Ibid., p. 28.

14 L. M. Mead, *The New Politics of Poverty: The Nonworking Poor in America*, Basic Books, 1992, pp. x, 12, 133, 145, 261.

15 See Belk, 'The human consequences of consumer culture', p. 69.

16 See Hochschild, *The Commercialization of Intimate Life*, pp. 213ff.

17 See *Sweden's New Social Democratic Model*, Compass, 2005, p. 32.

18 Frank Furedi, 'Consuming Democracy: activism, elitism and political apathy, at www.geser.net/furedi.html.

19 Neil Lawson, *Dare More Democracy*, Compass, c.2000, p. 18.

20 See www.politics.co.uk (accessed 1 Mar. 2005).

21 See Tom DeLuca, *The Two Faces of Political Apathy*, Temple University Press, 1995.

22 See Anders, *Die Antiquiertheit des Menschen*; here quoted from the French translation *L'Obsolescence de l'homme. Sur l'âme à l'époque de la deuxième révolution industrielle*, Éditions Inrea, 2001, pp. 30, 32.

Index